The Old School Project:

Historic Schools of Ottawa County Michigan

By Dana Kenneth Johnson

Foreword

Historic Schools of Ottawa County, Michigan, is the fourth installment in **The Old School Series** of books I've published on Michigan schools, the result of over 2000 hours of research and compilation, and over 2000 miles of driving to photograph the remaining schools in each county.

This book is organized alphabetically by township, of which Ottawa County has 17. Included is a simplified county map (next page) that provides context as to the relative locations of each respective township.

I've documented that some 150 schools have existed in Ottawa County and have confirmed that 75 or so are still standing. While maps and other references indicate school locations, they too often don't provide school names, so many remain unidentified. If you have such information, please e-mail me at DanaKennethJohnson@gmail.com or call
541-419-6491.

References and Resources

- Michigan School Database @ https://sites.rootsweb.com/%7Emivanbur/KentSchools.htm
- Michigan One-Room Schools database at https://michiganoneroomschoolhouses.blogspot.com/search?q=Kent+County
- Michigan One Room School Association @ www.miorsa.org
- Northwest Ottawa County Encyclopedia Of History, Vol. II - Buildings and Sites, 2017 by Wallace K. Ewing, Ph.D., Second electronic edition November 2018, Third electronic edition, August 2019
- Northwest Ottawa County Encyclopedia Of History, Vol. IV – Topics, Bibliography, 2017 by Wallace K. Ewing, Ph.D., Second electronic edition November 2018
- Standard Atlas of Ottawa County, Michigan, compiled and published by Geo. A. Ogle & Co., Chicago, 1912
- Illustrated Historical Atlas of the Counties of Ottawa & Kent, Michigan, H. Belden & Co., Chicago, 1873
- http://migenweb.org/ottawa/schools/
- Michigan County Atlas; Backroads & Forgotten Places, Universal Map by Kappa Map Group, 2017
- Michigan County Atlas; Backroads & Unforgettable Places, David M. Brown, Universal Map by Kappa Map Group, 2018

Ottawa County Townships

Allendale	Holland	Robinson
Blendon	Jamestown	Spring Lake
Chester	Olive	Tallmadge
Crockery	Park	Wright
Georgetown	Polkton	Zeeland
Grand Haven	Port Sheldon	

Ottawa County, 1873

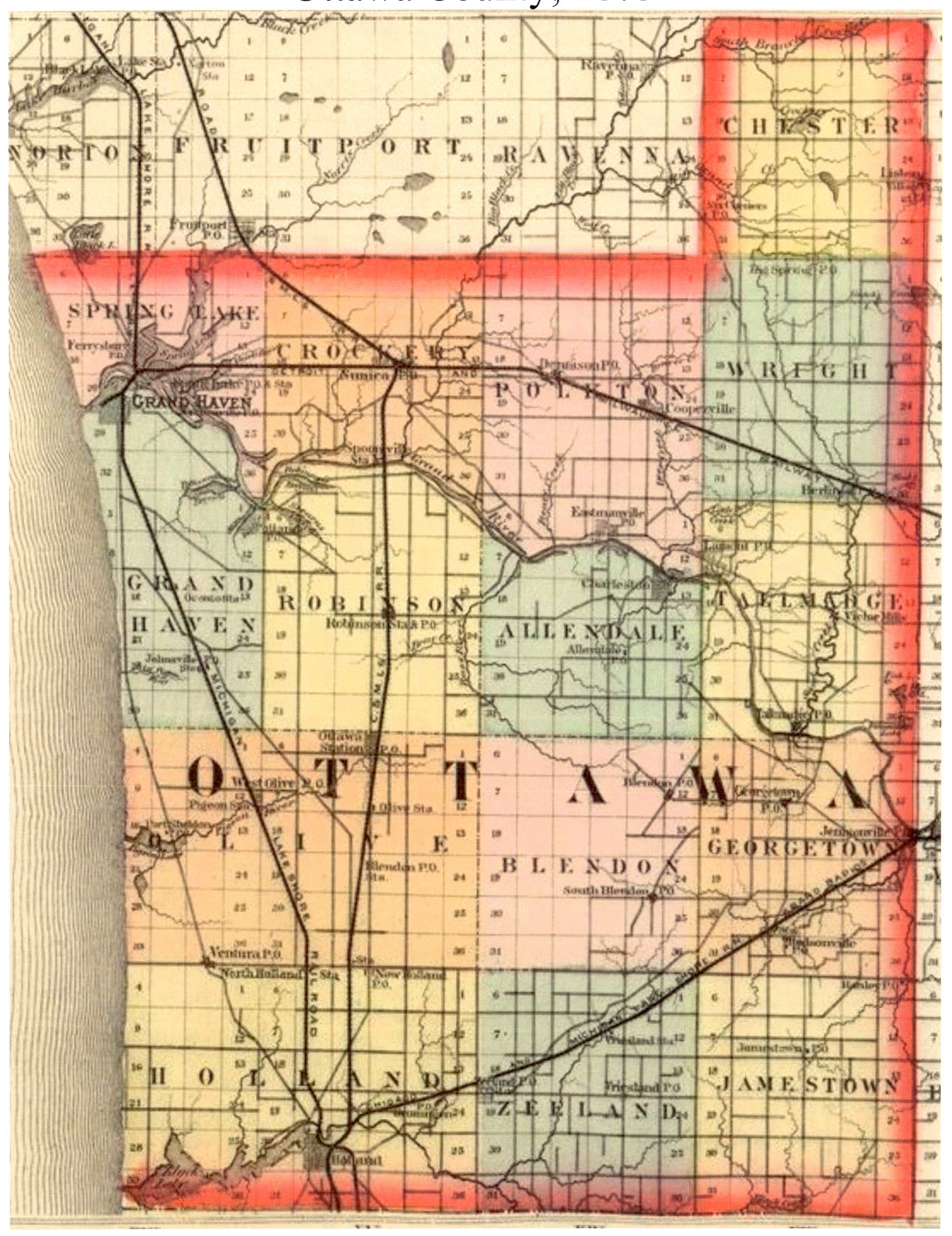

Ottawa County
Michigan Department of Natural Resources

Allendale Township

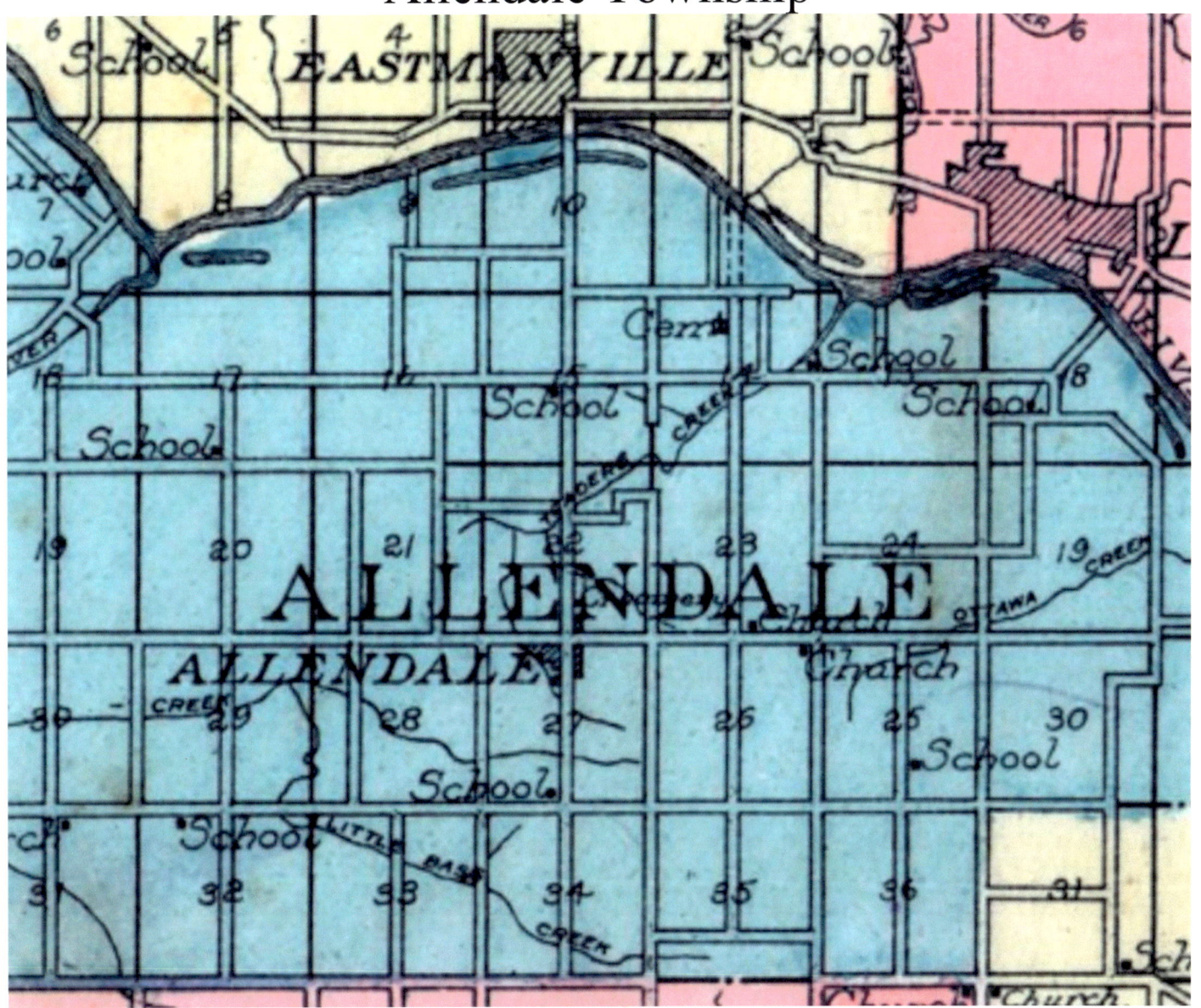

1912 map

Allendale Township Schools

School Name	District	Section	Location	Notes
Bass		7	W side River Rd N of Lincoln St	1912 map; No longer standing
Charleston?		14	NW cor Warner St & 56th Av, Charleston	1912 map; No longer standing
		15	SW cor Warner St & 68th Av	1912 map; No longer standing
		17	NW cor Buchanan & 84th	1912 map; No longer standing
	18E		N side Bliss @ 46th	1912 map; No longer standing
Allendale?		22	NE cor Lake Michigan (M-45) & 68th	1912 map; No longer standing
		25	E side 52nd S of Winfield	1912 map; Converted to residence
		27	10411 68th Av, NW cor Pierce & 68th	1912 map; Converted to residence

Allendale High		27	10760 68th Av, Allendale	Stanley Boven, Principal, Aug 28, 1936; Still in operation
Evergreen Elementary		27	10505 Learning Ln, Allendale	Currently operating
Springview Elementary		27	10505 Learning Ln, Allendale	Currently operating
Star		32	S side Pierce betw 84th & 88th	1912 map; Lois VanSomeren, teacher, Aug 28, 1936; Status unknown
Blakeney				Elsa M. Vannatter, teacher, August 28, 1936
Brotherton				Mrs. Mildred Scott, teacher, August 28, 1936
Curry				Enno Keegstra, teacher, August 28, 1936
Parish				Mary E. Wolbrink, teacher, August 28, 1936
Tuttle				
Van Westenberg				Dora Pertpstra Potts teacher, pd $40/month, boarded with local family $4/week, on weekends she traveled to her parents' home in Tallmadge Township; Closed by start of 1936 school year
White				Mrs. Doris Plant, teacher, August 28, 1936

Springview School and Evergreen Elementary School, 10505 Learning Ln, Allendale

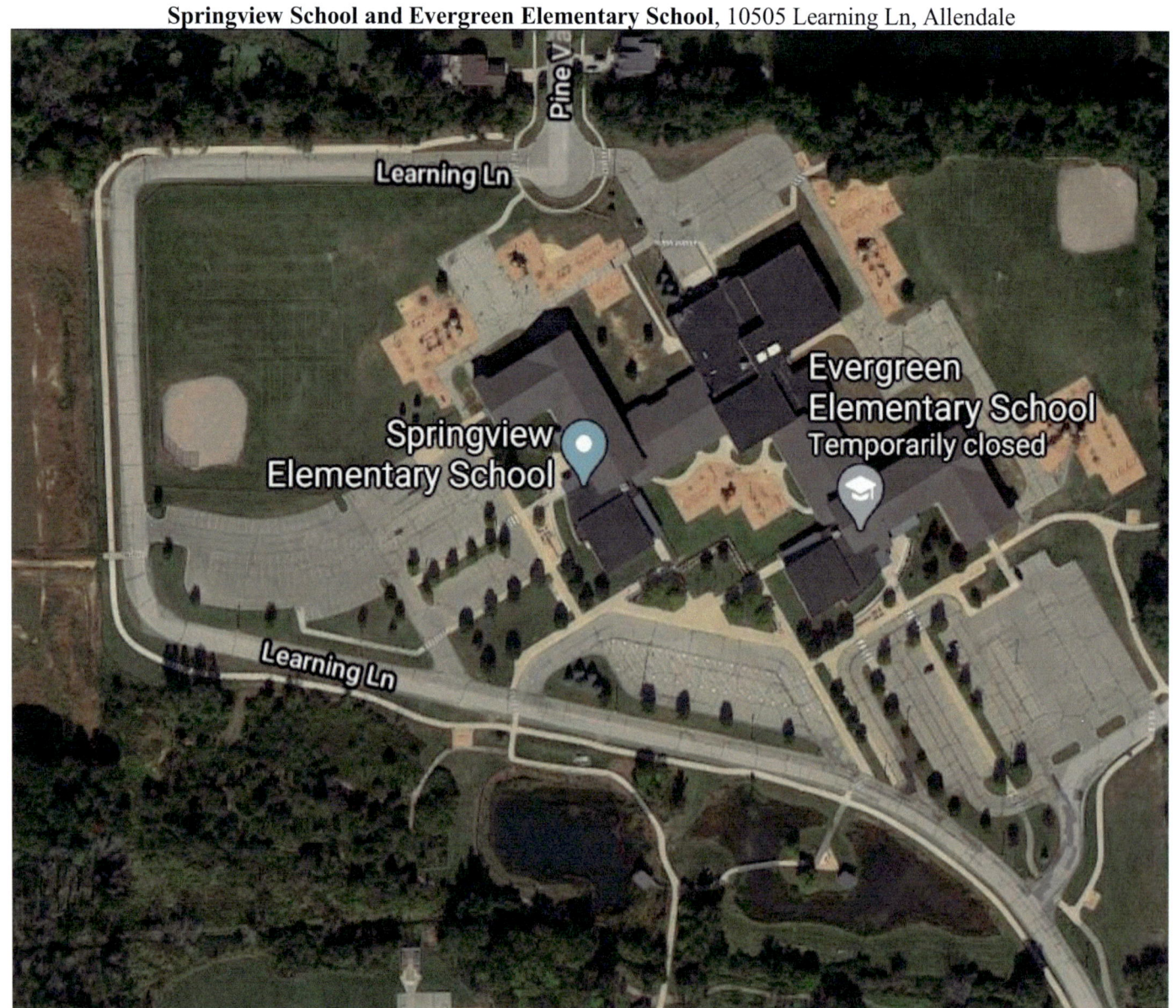

Image via Google

(Unidentified school), Allendale Township, Section 25, 10574 52nd Av, Allendale; E side of 52nd Av @ Windfield Dr

(Unidentified school), Allendale Township, Section 27, NW corner Pierce Rd & 68th Av

Blendon Township

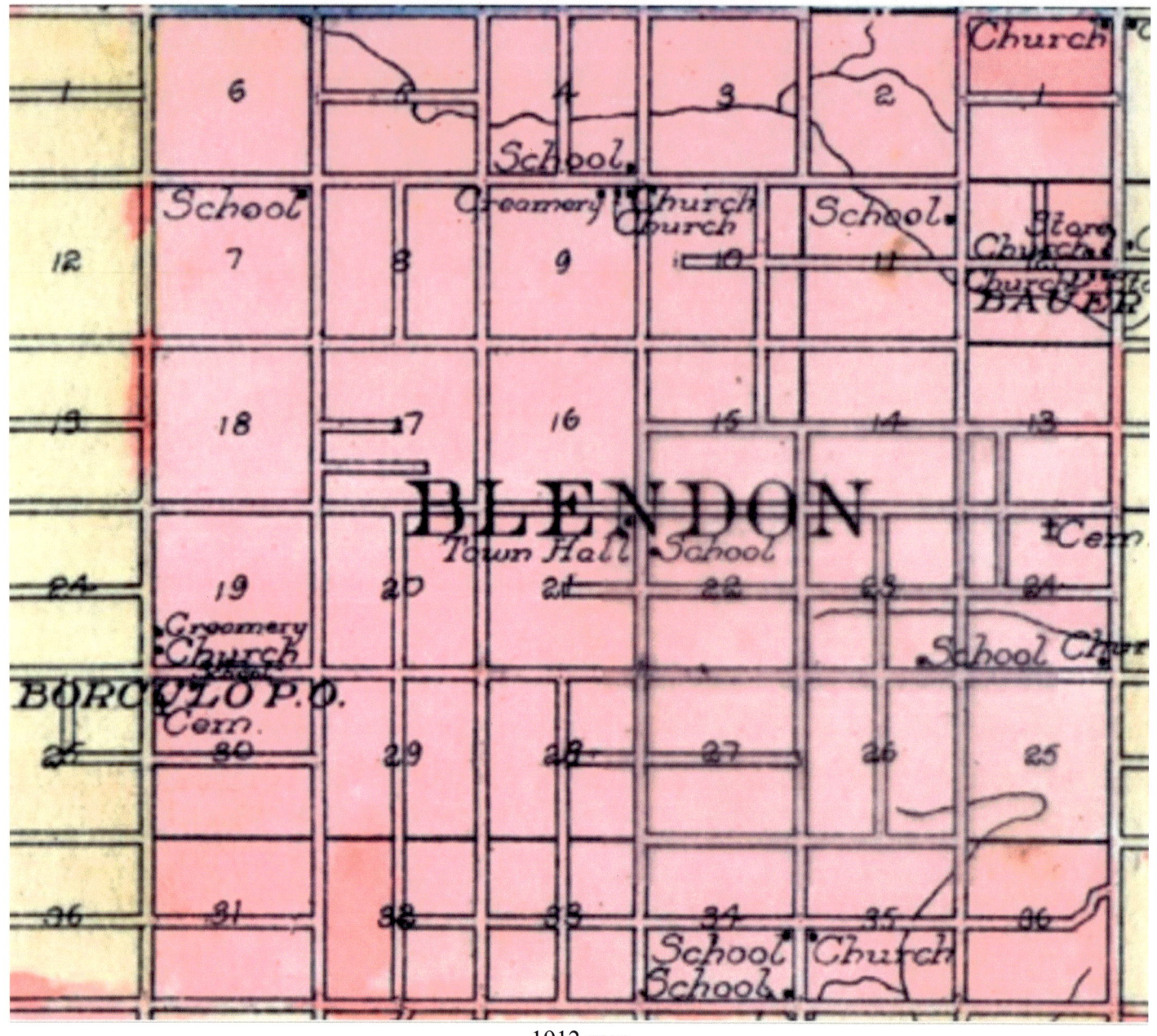

1912 map

Blendon Township Schools

School Name	District	Section	Location	Notes
North Blendon		4	NW cor Taylor & 72nd	1912 map; No longer standing
Eagle		7	SW cor Taylor & 88th	1912 map; Converted to residence
Blendon	1	11	SW cor 54th & Bauer	No longer standing
		22	SE cor Tyler & 72nd	No longer standing
South Blendon		23	5857 Port Sheldon Rd, N side Port Sheld St betw 56th & 60th	Converted to residence
Borculo / District 5	5	30	SE cor Port Sheldon & 96th	Restored & converted to event center in 2015
Sherbourne	4	34	NW cor New Holland & 64th	Converted to residence

1925 North Blendon School Class

Front Row: Harold Klinger, Claude Pikaart, Simon Dys, Chester Postma, David Berghorst, Russell Dalman, Willard Dys, Joseph Klinger, Fred Berghorst
2nd Row: Irene Haverdink, Mamie Klinger, Dora Berghorst, Anna Berghorst, Tena Styf, Katie Berghorst, Margaret Postma, Doris VanderMolen, Margaret Grant, Wilma Pikaart, Evelyn Pikaart, Henrietta Haverdink, Clara Dys, Stella Berghorst, Hilda Styf
3rd Row: Corrie Dalman, Henry Grant, Don Dalman, Frank Moll, Russel Berghorst, Andrew Lamar, Chester Dalman, Gerald Berghorst, Clarence Moll
Back Row: Simon Berghorst, John Dys, Ida Haverdink, Wes Swanson, teacher, Lavina Kuyers, Jennie Berghorst, Ella Dalman, Grace Berghorst, Marvin Dalman, Sebus Berghorst, Harold Haverdink, Edward Postma, Peter Moll, Henry Dys
Contributed by: Vicki Brovont
Created: 11 July 2011
URL: http://ottawa.migenweb.net/schools/blendon/1925NBlendon.html
Colorized using DeOldify from MyHeritage.com

Eagle School, Blendon Towmship, Section 7, SW corner Taylor & 88th

1912-1913 Blendon School District #1 Students

Back Row: Matilda Abel, teacher of Bauer Road, Reka Velthouse, Thora MacDonald, Mildred Dingeman, Ida Miedema, Oda Nibbelink, Catherine Behrens, Vesta Smedley, Marian Parady, Clara MacDonald, Johanna Jongekrijg, Earl Nibbelink, Darl Kautenberg, Bernard Engle

Third Row: Grace Dingeman, Clara Dekker, Frank Kautenberg, Harvey Behrens, Arthur Tambke, Henry Snoeyink, John Dekker, _____ Blue, Hazel Nibbelink, Henrietta Borgerding, John Snoeyink, Russell Haskins, Dorothy Tambke

Second Row: Charles Smedley, Nelson Dekker, Legar Dingeman, Arthur MacDonald, Walter Behrens, Gail Mosher, John Borgerding, Zwier Snoeyink, Helen Behrens, Ortha Mosher, Lila Seydel, Marie Borgerding, Leah Kautenberg

Front Row: Raymond Leestma, Clayton Blue, Julia Topp, Clara Butler, Gladys Seydel, Laura Nibbelink, Fred Snoeyink, Peter Borgerding, William Behrens, Floyd Lehman, Henry Borgerding, Frank Smedley, Marguerite Lehman

Blendon Township School No. 1 was located on Bauer Road at 56th Avenue. It closed in the 1950's with the consolidation of the schools and most of the students then went to the new Bauer Elementary School which is located on 48th Avenue, south of Bauer Road.

Scanned by ES
Created: 1 March 2006
URL: http://ottawa.migenweb.net/schools/blendon/1913No1Students.html
Colorized using DeOldify by MyHeritage.com

South Blendon School, Blendon Township, Sec 23, N side Port Sheldon St between 56th & 60th, circa 1920

In back row 2nd from right is Kenneth VanHeukelum (11/17/1913 – 12/30/2002) who graduated from Hudsonville High School in 1931.

Colorized using DeOldify by MyHeritage.com

South Blendon School, Blendon Township, Section 23, N side Port Sheldon St betw 56th & 60th, May 2020

1921 South Blendon District #2, Eighth Grade Graduation

Back Row: Henrietta Vruggink, Jennie Kort, Lena Wierenga, Elizabeth TerHaar, Jessie Kort, Henry VanderWall

Front Row: Marguerite VanHeukelum, Hazel Kunzi, Theresa Grandstra, George Vruggink, Gerrit Wierenga

Created: 1 March 2006
URL: http://ottawa.migenweb.net/schools/blendon/sbldn8grad.html 1
Colorized using DeOldify by MyHeritage.com

Borculo School, Blendon Township District #5, 9354 Port Sheldon Rd, Borculo; Sec 26, SE corner Port Sheldon & 96th, May 2020

Sherbourne School, Blendon Township District #4, Section 34, NW corner New Holland & 64th, 1917

Sherburne Eighth Grade Graduates, 1917
Back Row: Dina Wittengen Verbeek Westhuis, John Avink, _____ Zwagerman
Front Row: Winnie Luit, teacher Minnie Beld, Lawrence Klynstra

Colorized using DeOldify by MyHeritage.com

Sherbourne School, Blendon Township District #4, Section 34, NW corner New Holland & 64th, May 2020

Beaverdam Christian School, Blendon Towmship, District #5, Section 35, SE corner Barry & 64th, 1959

Libertas (Beaverdam) Christian School, Blendon Towmship, District #5, Section 35, SE corner Barry & 64th, May 2020

Chester Township

1912 map

Chester Township Schools

School Name	District	Section	Location	Notes
Porter		2	N side Truman betw 8th & 16th	1876 & 1912 maps; Named for G F Porter who owned 120 acres and Mrs. H. porter who owned 40 acres nearby in 1876; Jean Ewing, teacher, Aug 28, 1936; Converted to residence
Harrisburg		5	NE cor Truman St & 36th Av	1912 map; Lucille Brydges, teacher, Aug 28, 1936; Unknown whether current house contains any elements of schoolhouse
Lachman		15	NW cor Gooding & 16th	1912 map; Named for W. Lachman who owned 80 acres nearby in 1876; Closed prior to 1936; Still standing
McNitt		17	NE cor Gooding & 40th	1912 map; Named for J. McNitt who owned 240 acres nearby in 1876; Edward Kelly, Jr, teacher, Aug 28, 1936; No longer standing
(Unknown)		22	W side 16th ¼ mi N of Coolidge	1912 map; Status unknown
Lisbon		25	NE cor Harding & 8th	1912 map; Mrs. Josephine Beuschel, teacher, Aug 28, 1936; No longer standing
Waller		27	SE cor Coolidge & 24th	1912 map; Named for D. Waller who owned 80 acres nearby in 1876; Still standing
Conklin		31	SW cor Harding & 40th	1912 map; Otto W. Hecksel, principal, Marvin TenElshof, Constance Hillman, Edith Fritz, teachers, Aug 28, 1936; No longer standing
Big Springs		33	NW cor Wilson & 24th	1912 map; Converted to residence

Porter School, Chester Township, Section 2, N side Truman between 8th & 16th, May 2020

Harrisburg School, Chester Township, Section 5, NE corner Truman & 36th, May 2020

Lachman School, Chester Township, Section 15, NW corner Gooding & 16th (Ken Talsma photo)

Image via Google

Waller School, Chester Township, Section 27, SE corner Coolidge & 24th, May 2020

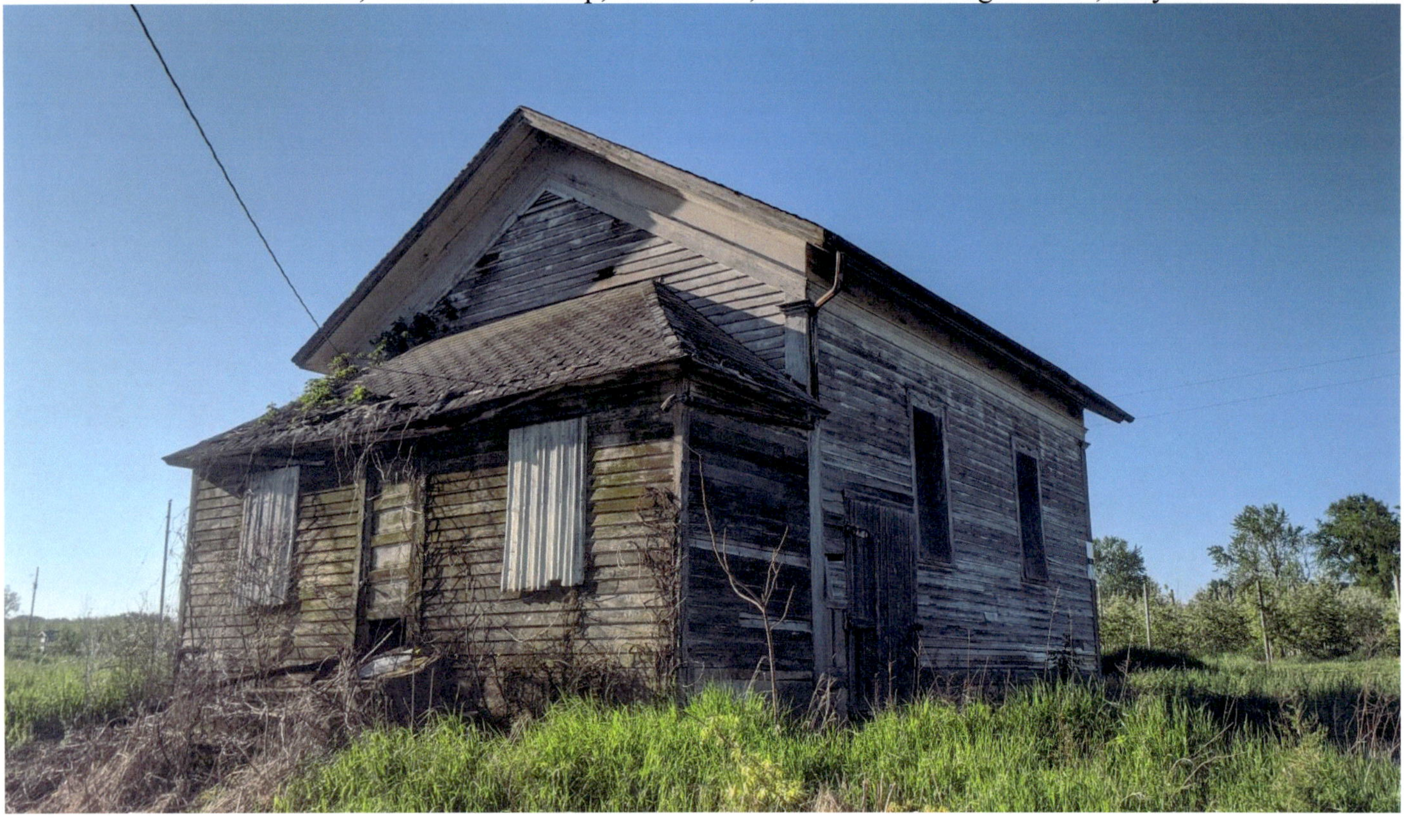

Big Spring School, Chester Township, Section 33, NW corner Wilson & 24th, May 2020

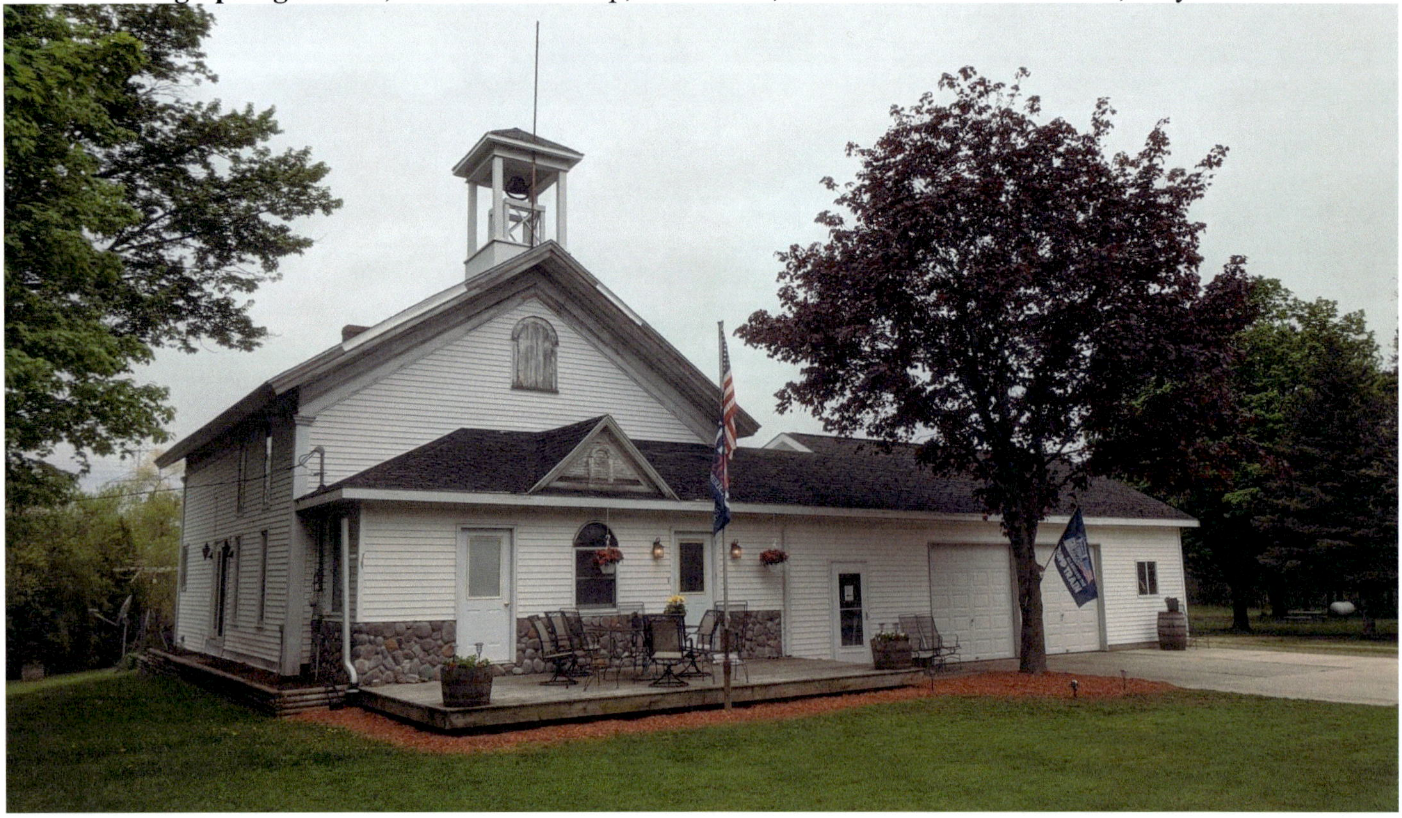

Crockery Township

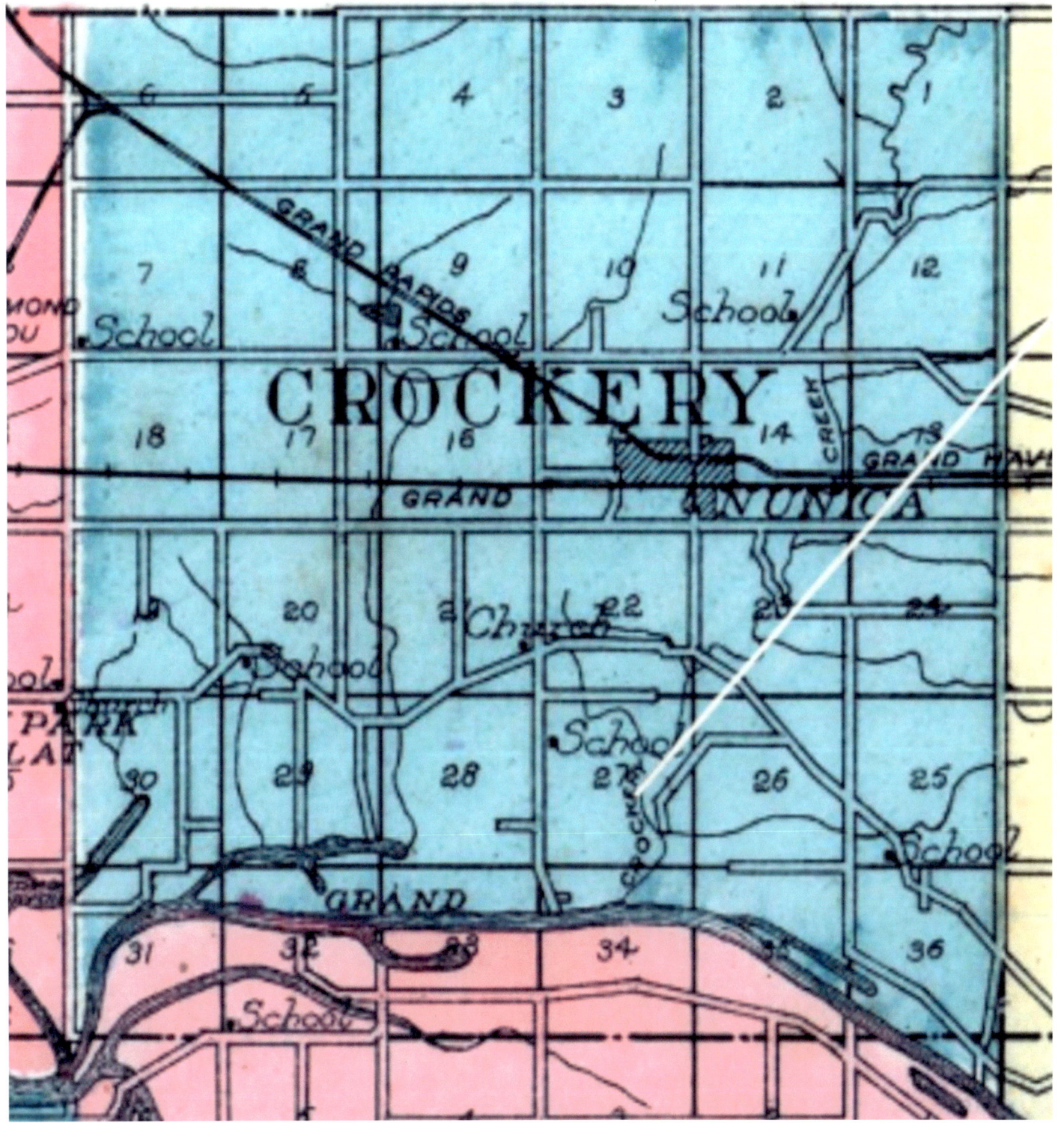

1912 map

Crockery Township Schools

School Name	District	Section	Location	Notes
McMann		7	14389 State Rd, Nunica; NE cor State Rd & 144th	A Spring Lake School established in 1856 & named for Jeremiah & Ellen (North) McMann who donated the land for the school; Later became part of Fruitport school system; Mrs. Marval Lund, teacher, Aug 28, 1936; Last served as a church
		9	N side State Rd near Apple Rd	1912 map; No longer standing
		11	W side Walnut N of State Rd	1912 map; Status unconfirmed
Taylor		20	SE cor Leonard St & 136th	Organized in 1849 and named for its 1st teacher; Converted to residence; No longer standing
Patchin		20	E side 136th S of Cleveland	District organized in 1855; School named for landowner J. Manley Patchin who owned 40 acres in Section 20; District reorganized in 1855, and a second schoolhouse was built in 1856 on S side Leonard near 130th; Remodeled during 1933-34 school year; Raised for basement added in 1938; Merged with Spring Lake School District in 1957; Converted to residence
		24	W side 96th @ Arthur	1912 map; No longer standing
		25	SW side Leonard E of Garfield	1912 map; 10037 Leonard St, Coopersville
		25	SW side Leonard NW of 100th	10060 Leonard St, Coopersville, Mustard Vernon L Clu Farm; Built on Leonard Road just west of 100th Avenue
Spoonville		27	E side 120th, 1 mi S of Arthur, ½ mi N of Spoonville	1912 map; John Spoon founded a mill at Spoonville in 1856; Status unknown
Crockery / Nunica		22	11741 Leonard; N side Leonard betw 112th & 120th, now Terra Verde Golf Course	One-room frame building was purchased from Spoonville School Board in 1864 and used until 1875 when new schoolhouse was built; Original was moved and used as a German church; 2nd school was used until 1956; Used as a storage facility until 1998 when Bonnie Corbin spotted the abandoned building and purchased it from Gerald Pitcher with the intention of making it their residence
Indian		31	E side 144th @ Battle Point Site	Organized by Leo Lillie for local Native Americans at Battle Point; Methodist Episcopal pastor Rev. Bartlett established the school in 1855
French				Ferris Hering, teacher, Aug 28, 1936
Lawrence				Eli O'Bradovich, teacher, Aug 28, 1936

McMann School, Crockery Township, Section 7, NE corner State Rd & 144th, May 2020

(Unidentified School), Crockery Township, Section 9, N side State Rd between 130th & Apple Dr, May 2020

(Unidentified School), Crockery Township, Section 11, W side Walnut N of State Rd, May 2020

(Unidentified School), Crockery Twp, Sec 25, 10060 Leonard St, Coopersville

Site of 2nd Patchin School, Crockery Township, Section 29, 13010 Leonard, S side Leonard @ 130th

Georgetown Township

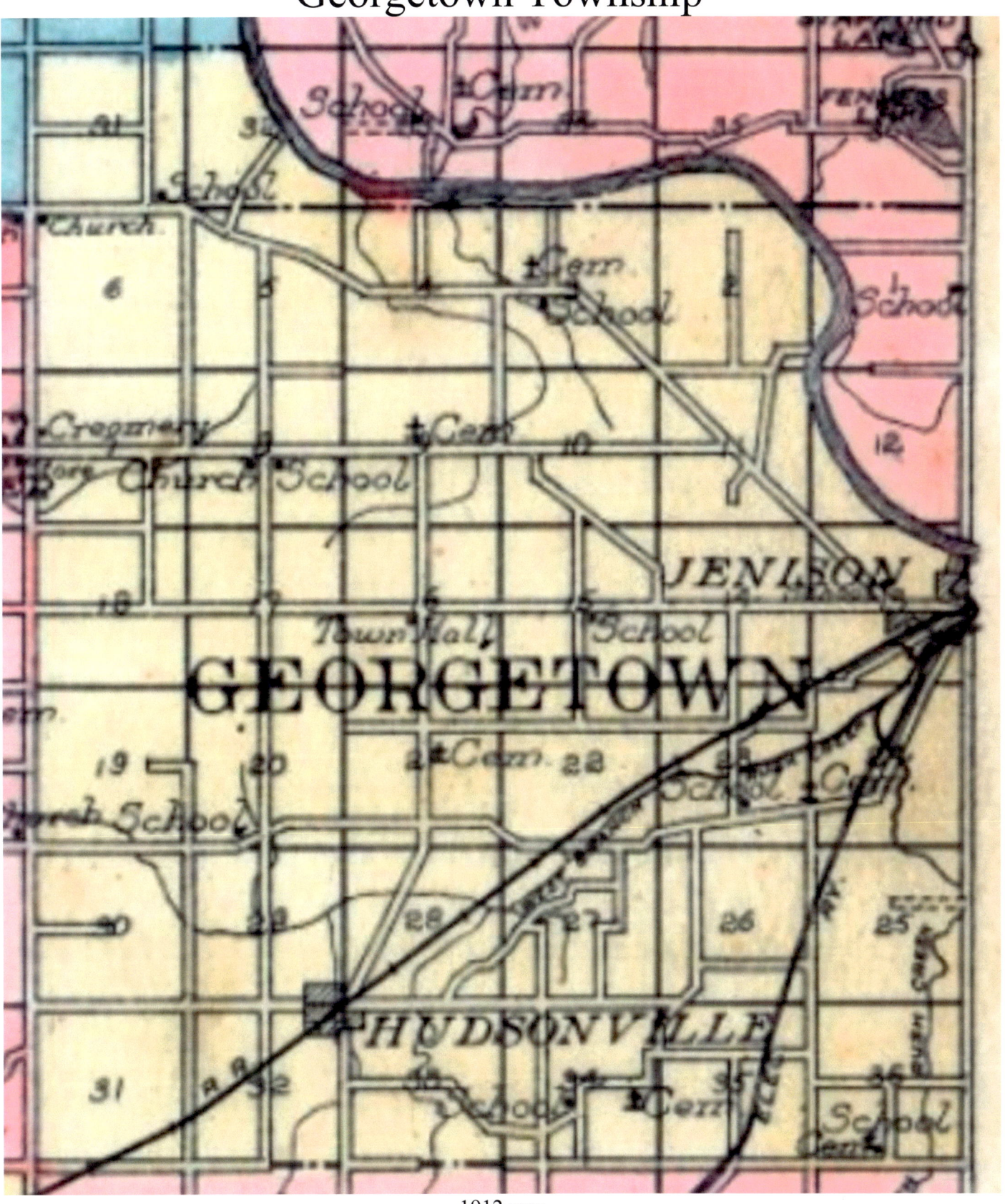

1912 map

Georgetown Township Schools

School Name	District	Section	Location	Notes
		3	S side Fillmore @ 22nd	1912 map; No longer standing
Bauer		7	8269 48th Av, Hudsonville, E side 48th ¼ mi S of Bauer Rd	Converted to residence?
Bauer Elementary		7	E side 48th ¼ mi S of Bauer Rd	Still in operation
Canada Hill	1	8	SE cor Bauer & 36th	1912 map; Built in the 1860's. A group of immigrants from Canada migrated to Georgetown Township and this may be where the school got its name. With the consolidation of schools in the 1950s, the schoolhouse was closed in 1957. In 1958, it became the home of the Georgetown Grange. The students from Canada Hill then went to Bauer Elementary School which was built to also accommodate the students from Blendon School No. 1; Arthur DeVries, Helen Bosink, teachers, Aug 28, 1936; Converted to residence
		13	NE side Cottonwood Dr & N of Baldwin St	1912 map; No longer standing
Sandy Hill / Sand Hill		15	SE cor Baldwin & 20th	1912 map; Mrs. Martha Hoag, teacher, Aug 28, 1936; Still operating as elementary school
Alward		20	NW cor Port Sheldon & 36th	1912 map; Dennis Roelofs, Margaret Repic, teachers, Aug 28, 1936; Still operating as an elementary school
Bursley		23	NE cor Port Sheldon & 12th	1912 map; The original building wa a log cabin at 8th Avenue; A one-room frame school was built on the present site around 1837, replaced in 1950 with current building (Ottawa.migenweb.net/schools/georgetw/Bursley.html); Francis Tigelaar, Hazel Northouse, teachers, Aug 28, 1936
Bursley Elementary		23	NE cor Port Sheldon & 12th	1950-present, operating as elementary school
Chrysler		31	NE cor Fillmore & 42nd	M1igenweb.org/ottawa/schools/georgetw/Chrysler.html
Shackhuddle	8	34	2091 Barry, Hudsonville	Built in 1930; Previous structure burned down in 1928; Converted to residence
Haire				Albert Spyker, teacher, Aug 28, 1936
Hanley				Ezra Balzer, teacher, Aug 28, 1936
Jenison				Clay Utter, teacher, Aug 28, 1936
Hudsonville High				D. H. VandeBunte, Superintendent; Francis Geuge, Principal; Gerrit Brandt, Ruth VerHey, Faith Fleser, Don VanVoorhorst, Myrtle Klooster, Gladys Seydell, Norma Alward, teachers, Aug 28, 1936

Chrysler School, Georgetown Township, Section 3, NE corner Fillmore & 42nd, date unknown

Bauer School, Georgetown Township, Section 7, E side 48th S of Bauer Rd, 1890s

Bauer School site, 8269 48th, Hudsonville, Georgetown Township, Section 7, E side 48th S of Bauer Rd

Sandy Hill Elementary School, Georgetown Township, Section 15, SE corner Baldwin & 20th, May 2020

Alward Elementary School, Georgetown Township, Section 20, N side Port Sheldon between 36th & 40th, May2020

Alward Elementary School Students - circa 1910
Includes students, Gladys Gerrits (12/07/1904 - 01/30/1993) and Henrietta Brink

Colorized using DeOldify by MyHeritage.com

Bursley School, Georgetown Township, Section 23, NE corner Port Sheldon & 12th, end of 1898 school year

Colorized using DeOldify by MyHeritage.com

Bursley Elementary School, Georgetown Township, Section 23, NE corner Port Sheldon & 12th, May 2020

Shackhuddle School, 2091 Barry, Hudsonville, Georgetown Township District 8, circa 1910

Shackhuddle One-Room Schoolhouse, circa 1910

Back Row: _____, Robert McCoy, John Schut, Laura Boldt, Lucy Drew, Clarence Talsma, Pete Talsma, Harold Schut, Morrill Gate, Jim Schut

Middle Row: _____, Edna Schut, Ada VanderMolen, Mabel Schut, May Smith, Mary Besteman, Edith Talsma, Nella Smith, Dena Besteman

Front Row: Julius Gerrits, Lee VanderMolen, Jim Besteman, _____, Bill Talsma, _____, Lawrence Mesbergen, Jim VanderMolen, Harry Boldt, Chuck Hemshaw

Colorized using DeOldify by MyHeritage.com

Shackhuddle School, 2091 Barry, Hudsonville, Georgetown Township District 8, May 2020

Canada Hill School, Georgetown Township, District #1, Section 8, SE corner Bauer & 36th, 1925

CANADA HILL SCHOOL (2 Room, K - 8) near Hudsonville, Mi. 1925

8th grade Graduation, Canada Hill School, near Hudsonville, MI. 1929
Back Row: Henry Abel (cousin), Margerite Isenga, Nelly Alberda
Front Row: Edward VanHarn, John Abel, Anna Lemmink

Grand Haven Township

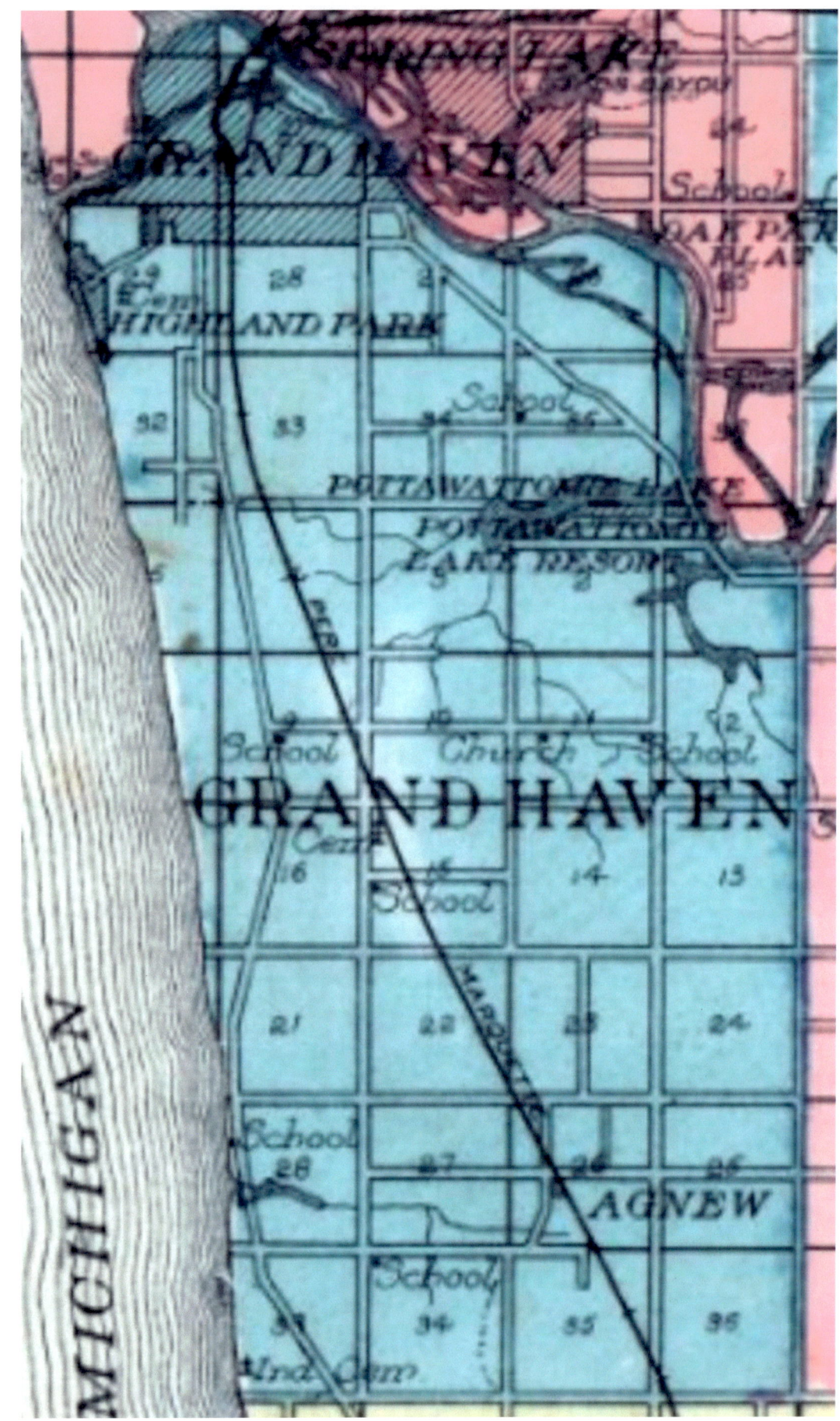

1912 map

Grand Haven Township Schools

School Name	District	Section	Location	Notes
Rosy Mound		9	SE cor Lake Shore Av & Ferris	An acre of land was purchased for the school on Mar 23, 1861; Burned down on Jan 9, 1900; Moved to Section 4 in 1911; Rosy Mound Elementary School now located at SE cor Lake Shore Dr & Rosy Mound Rd
Bignell		11	SW cor Ferris & 152nd, Grand Haven (1912 map)	Converted to private residence at 15318 Ferris St, Grand Haven, purchased by Tim Travis in 2020
unconfirmed		14	15230 Lincoln St; SW cor Lincoln & 152nd	House resembles one-room school, status unconfirmed
German Lutheran		15	SE cor Warner & 168th (1912 map)	Served as township hall until the mid-1950s; Converted to residence; Greatly renovated between 2015 & 2020
Central		20	Block of 6th, 7th, Clinton & Franklin, Grand Haven	Central School complex still stands on site
Beech Tree / Beechtree		27	NE cor Pennoyer & Beechtree, Grand Haven	Built in 1881 at what is now Bolt Park; Closed at end of school year Spring 1913; Purchased in 1916 by Otto Glueck and moved to 1511 Pennoyer; Converted to residence
Salvator Tomaso?		28	W side Lake Shore Av betw Pierce & Lake Michigan Dr (1912 map)	No longer standing
Peach Plains Elementary		35(N)	15849 Comstock Rd; NE cor Comstock & 160th	1st school built between 1864 & 1876; New school built in 1922; A 4-classroom brick building was constructed in 1953; 4 more classrooms added in 1956; 1959 addition accommodated a kitchen, multipurpose room, office space & 6 more classrooms; Merged with Grand Haven school system in June 1961; East wing built in 1964 housed media center and several more classrooms; A 1990 addition allotted more space for media center and another classroom
Columbus / 2nd Ward			128 Columbus, Grand Haven	Built in 1881; Torn down in 1930; Office building now stands on site
Elliott Elementary			601 Elliott St, Grand Haven; NE cor Elliott & 6th	Opened in 1963 for Kindergarten to 2nd Grade; Converted to alternative education site in 1976; Now operates as Ottawa Area Intermediate School District @ 605 Elliott
1st Street / Select			Lot 70, 121 S 1st St, Grand Haven; NE cor Clinton & 1st	Built in 1836; No longer standing
2nd Street			Lot 186, 2nd St N of Franklin, Grand Haven	Built prior to 1836; Grand Haven's 1st school, also used as public meeting house, church, public building, courthouse, and school for Mary A. White's classes until replaced by 1st Street School
Ferry / 4th Ward / Voyager			SW cor Ferry & Pennoyer	Opened in September 1913 as 4th Ward School, replacing smaller Beech Tree School; Now operates as Voyager and Ferry School
Grand Haven Christian			606 Jackson St, Grand Haven	Small, frame building, built in 1867 at 413 Columbus, was moved in 1872 to 707 Jackson Street, serving 1st as a church; Grand Haven

				Christian School was founded in 1880; City of Grand Haven purchased the building in 1883 to operate as public school
Grand Haven Christian			513 Jackson St, Grand Haven	William Baker donated land to Grand Haven Christian School where a small school was built and opened on December 1, 1883, and operated until 1950 when a new school was built at 1102 Grant on September 6 1950
Grand Haven Christian			1102 Grant, Grand Haven	Groundbreaking Sept 6, 1950, Classes started Sept 1951, dedication Apr 19, 1953; Still in operation
Grand Haven High			7th St, Grand Haven	1st high school opened September 1922; 2nd high school built in 1938 on land owned by the school board near the south end of 7th Street in an area called Green Hill; 1st school was used as Jr. High until razed in 1967 when new Jr. High opened on Griffin Street; New high school campus opened in 1997on corner of Ferris St & US-31
Griffin Elementary			1700 S Griffin, Grand Haven	Built in 1967 to relieve Ferry School of some of its student population, serving kindergarten through sixth grade
Jackson Street			606 Jackson Street, Grand Haven	Wood frame structure constructed in 1867 at 413 Columbus by congregation of the First Christian Reformed Church and moved to this site in 1872; Operated as African American Church for a few years; Opened as public school in 1883; No longer standing
Mary A White Elementary			1400 Wisconsin Av, Grand Haven	Built in 1959; Named after Grand Haven's 1st teacher, Mary Arms White; Efforts to name a school after her were underway as early as September 1922; Still in operation
Monroe Street			Monroe betw 5th & 6th, Grand Haven	Operated in the 1800s; No longer standing
St. Patrick's			920 Fulton St, Grand Haven	Opened in 1919; Still in operation
Stone			1720 S Beechtree St, Grand Haven; NE cor Robbins Rd & Beechtree/168th Av	Opened in 1900 to alleviate concerns over children crossing railroad tracks to attend Rosy Mound School; Operated until 1962; Now serves as Kid's Court Child Care & Preschool
Union / Clinton Street			106 S 6th St, Grand Haven; framed by Franklin & Clinton, 6th & 7th	Opened in 1860; Site now occupied by Central School

Elliott School, Grand Haven Township, 601 Elliott, Grand Haven (now Ottawa Area ISD @ 605 Elliott)

St Patrick's School, Grand Haven Township, 897 Fulton, Grand Haven

Grand Haven Christian School, Grand Haven Township, 1102 Grant Av, Grand Haven

Mary A. White School, Grand Haven Township, 1400 Wisconsin Av, Grand Haven

Bignell School, Grand Haven Township, 15318 Ferris St, Grand Haven

Photo credit: Tim Travis, 2021

Photo credit: Zillow.com, 2020

Rosy Mound Elementary School, Grand Haven Township, Section 4, SE corner Lakeshore & Rosy Mound

(Unidentified School?) Grand Haven Township, Section 14, SW corner Lincoln & 152nd

German Lutheran School, Grand Haven Township, Section 15, SE corner Warner & 168th
August 2015 via Google

German Lutheran School, Grand Haven Township, Section 15, SE corner Warner & 168th
May 2020

Central High School, Grand Haven Township, Section 20, Block of 6th, 7th, Clinton & Franklin, Grand Haven

Beecchtree School, Grand Haven Township, Section 27, NE corner Beechtree & Pennoyer, Grand Haven

Peach Plains School, Grand Haven Township, Section 35, NE corner Comstock & 160th, 1909

Colorized using DeOldify from MyHeritage.com

Peach Plains Elementary School, Grand Haven Township, Section 35, NE corner Comstock & 160th, 2020

Columbus Street / Second Ward School, Grand Haven Township, Grand Haven, 1912 map

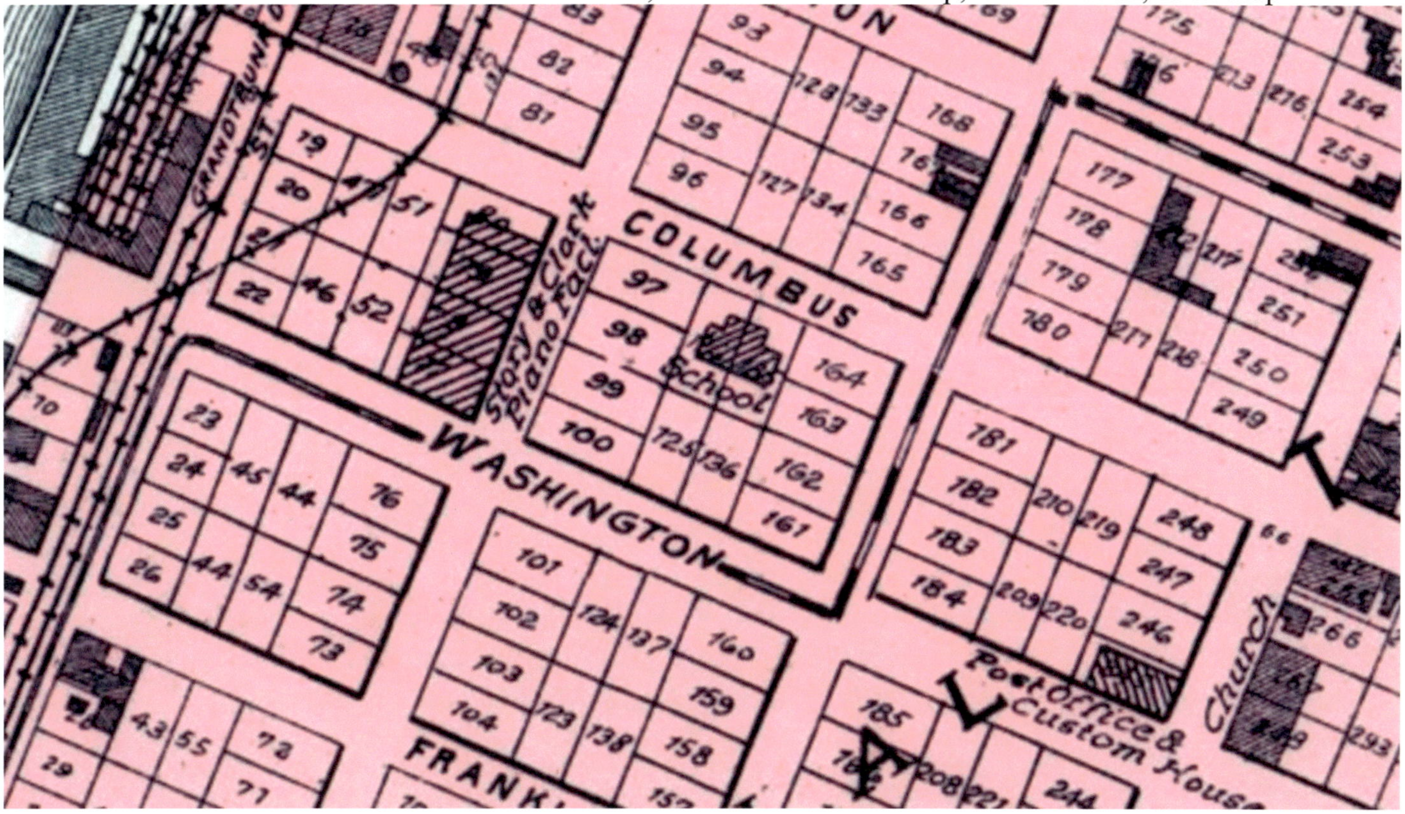

Columbus Street / Second Ward School, Grand Haven Township, Grand Haven

Ferry / Fourth Ward School, Grand Haven Township, SW corner Ferry & Pennoyer, Grand Haven

Holland (and future Park) Township, 1912

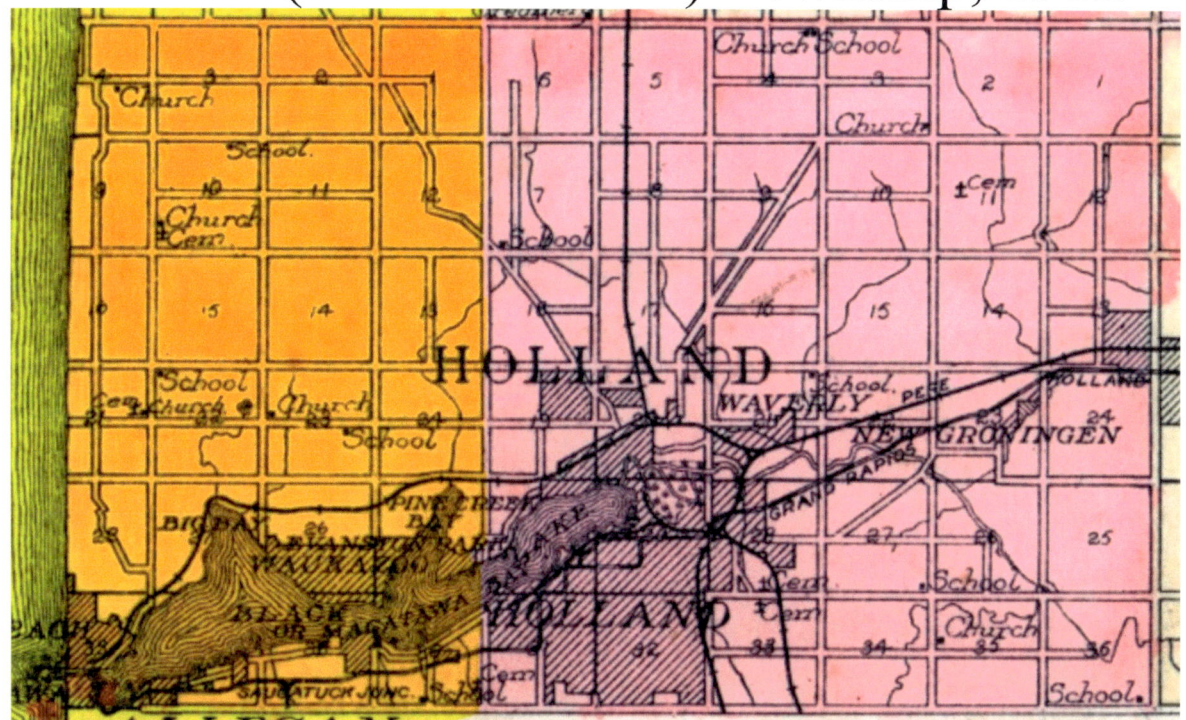

Park Township, highlighted in yellow, split from Holland Township in 1915.

Holland Township Schools

School Name	District	Section	Location	Notes
New Holland		3	SE cor New Holland & 120th	Now occupied by North Holland Elementary School
Sherwoods Mills?		7	NW cor Riley & 142nd	Now occupied by Boys & Girls Club of Holland
Pine Creek Elementary (West Ottawa Schools)		7	1184 136th, Holland	Currently operating
Macatawa Bay Middle School (West Ottawa Schools)		7	3700 140th, Holland	Currently operating
Harbor Lights Middle School (West Ottawa Schools)		7	1024 136th, Holland	Currently operating
New Groningen		14	10573 Paw Paw Dr, Zeeland	1881-1952; purchased in 2005 by Zeeland Historical Society; Opened as Museum 2011
		15	NE cor Greenly & 40th	No longer standing
District No. 4	4	27	370 Country Club Rd; NW cor 16th (Adams) & 112th (Country Club Rd), Holland (1912 map)	District No. 4, 1882 – 1928; Now houses Building Men for Life
Holland High		31	S side 24th betw Lugers & 136th (2017 map)	Currently operating

| Maple Grove / Longfellow | | | 24th Av near Central St | The original school was built in 1906 and given the name Maple Grove School. In 1916, the Holland Public School Board decided that all the school buildings be named for an historical figure. Maple Grove was renamed Longfellow Elementary School after Henry Wadsworth Longfellow. In the 1960s, an addition was built around the original structure. In the 1990s, a gymnasium and other classrooms were added. It later became a 4-5 Focus School. There is a Longfellow Tree which displays photos of the staff as far back as 1906. A centennial celebration had been planned, but the Holland Public School Board of Education made the decision that this school would close at the end of the 2006 school year due to budget constraints. |

Holland High School, Holland Township, S side 24th between Lugers & 136th, Holland

Undated postcard

Maple Grove / Longfellow School, Holland Township, 24th Av near Central St, Holland, built in 1906

North Holland Elementary School, Holland Twp, Sec 3, SE cor New Holland @ 120th, May 2020

Pine Creek / Sherwood Mills School? Now **Boys & Girls Club of Holland**, Holland Township, Section 7, NE corner Riley & Butternut, Holland
May 2020

1930

New Groningen School, Holland Township, Section 23, 10573 Paw Paw Dr, Zeeland, 2005

1934

New Groningen School, Holland Township, Section 23, 10573 Paw Paw Dr, Zeeland

(purchased by Zeeland Historica;l Society 2005

New Groningen School, Holland Township, Section 23 (1881-1952)

May 2020

District #4 School, 370 Country Club Rd, Holland; NW corner 16th (Adams) & 112th (Country Club Rd)

Jamestown Township, 1912

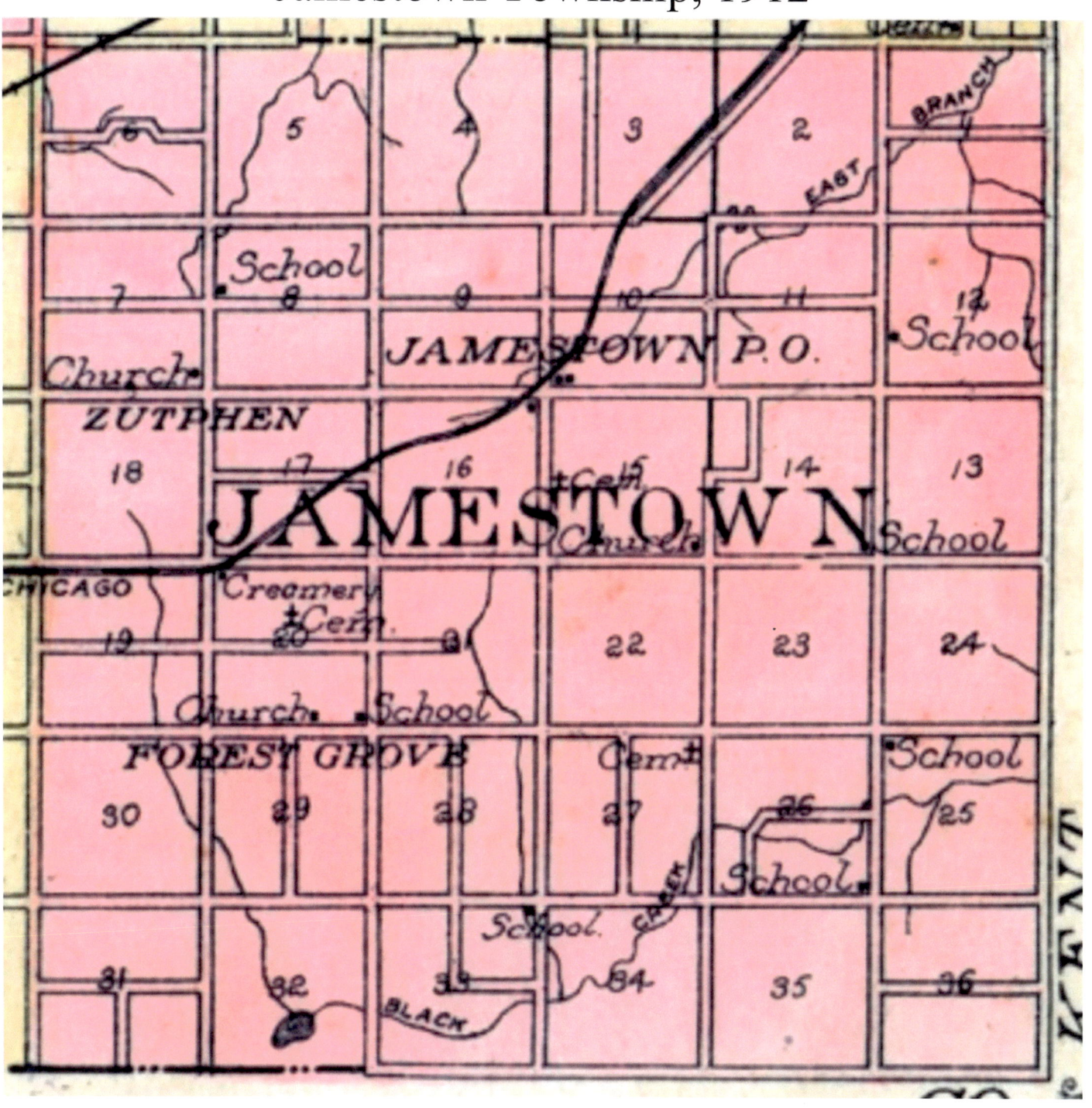

Jamestown Township Schools

School Name	District	Section	Location	Notes
Zutphen	5	8	NE cor Greenly & 40th, Zutphen	Two rooms; In operation 1867-1963; Fanny Wyma, Dorothy Postma, teachers, Aug 28, 1936; Converted to garage / farm storage
Jamestown Upper Elementary		9	3291 Lincoln St, Jamestown (Hudsonville)	
Riley Street Middle		9	2745 Riley St, Jamestown (Hudsonville)	
Bell	1F	12	3390 8th Av, Hudsonville; E side 8th S of Greenly (1912 map)	Mrs. Dorothy Horton, teacher, Aug 28, 1936; Converted to residence
Star	8	14	NW cor Byron & 8th (1912 map)	Still standing, abandoned; Mrs. Francis Buege. Teacher, Aug 28, 1936
Jamestown High	2	15	Jamestown (Hudsonville)	Built in Spring 1919; John Wyma, Principal; Henrietta Smeelink, Zora VanOsa, teachers, Aug 28, 1936
Forest Grove		20	NW cor Perry & 32nd (1912 map)	Bernard Klein—ker, Marie Hildebrandt, teachers, Aug 28, 1936; now Forest Grove Elementary School
Maple Grove	3	20		
West Grove / West	7	20		Kenneth Rynbrandt, teacher, Aug 28, 1936
Hilzey		25	SE cor Perry & 8th (1912 map)	Converted to residence
Mitchell	4	26	NW cor Adams & 8th (1912 map)	Raymond Brummel, teacher, Aug 28, 1936; Converted to residence
DeKline?		30	E side 48th ¾ mi N of Adams (1912 map)	Converted to residence
Gitchel	6	33	SW cor 24th Av & Adams St, Gitchel (1912 map)	In operation 1874–1957; Jessie DeJonge, teacher, Aug 28, 1936; Converted to residence

Zutphen School 1929 8th Grade Graduates, Jamestown Township District #5
Section 8, NE corner Greenly & 40th

Zutphen School, Jamestown Township District #5, Section 8, NE corner Greenly & 40th, May 2020

Bell School, Jamestown Township District #1F, Section 12, 3390 8th Av, Hudsonville

Star School, Jamestown Township District #8, Section 14, NW corner Byron & 8th, photo by Marsha Heyboer

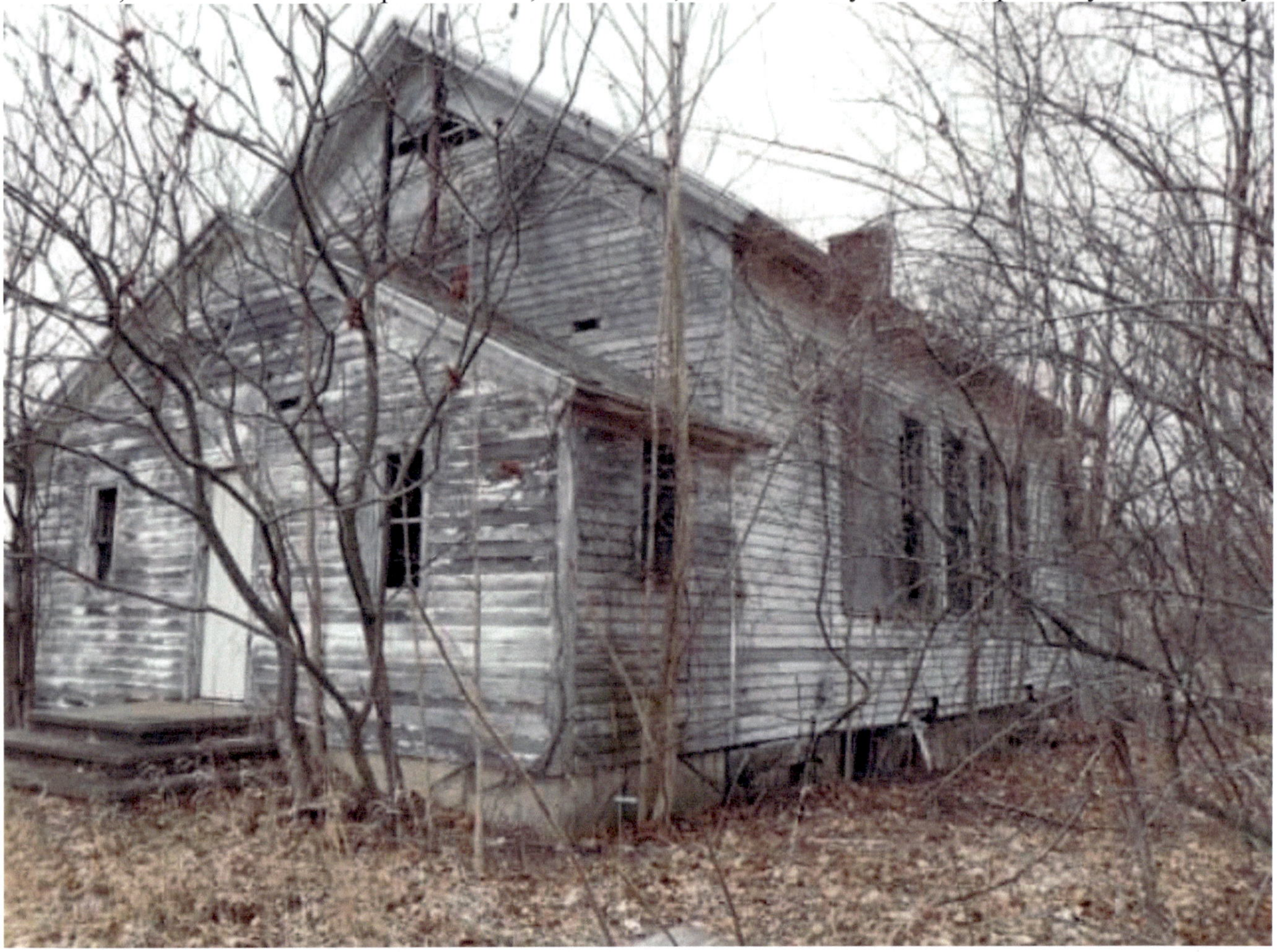

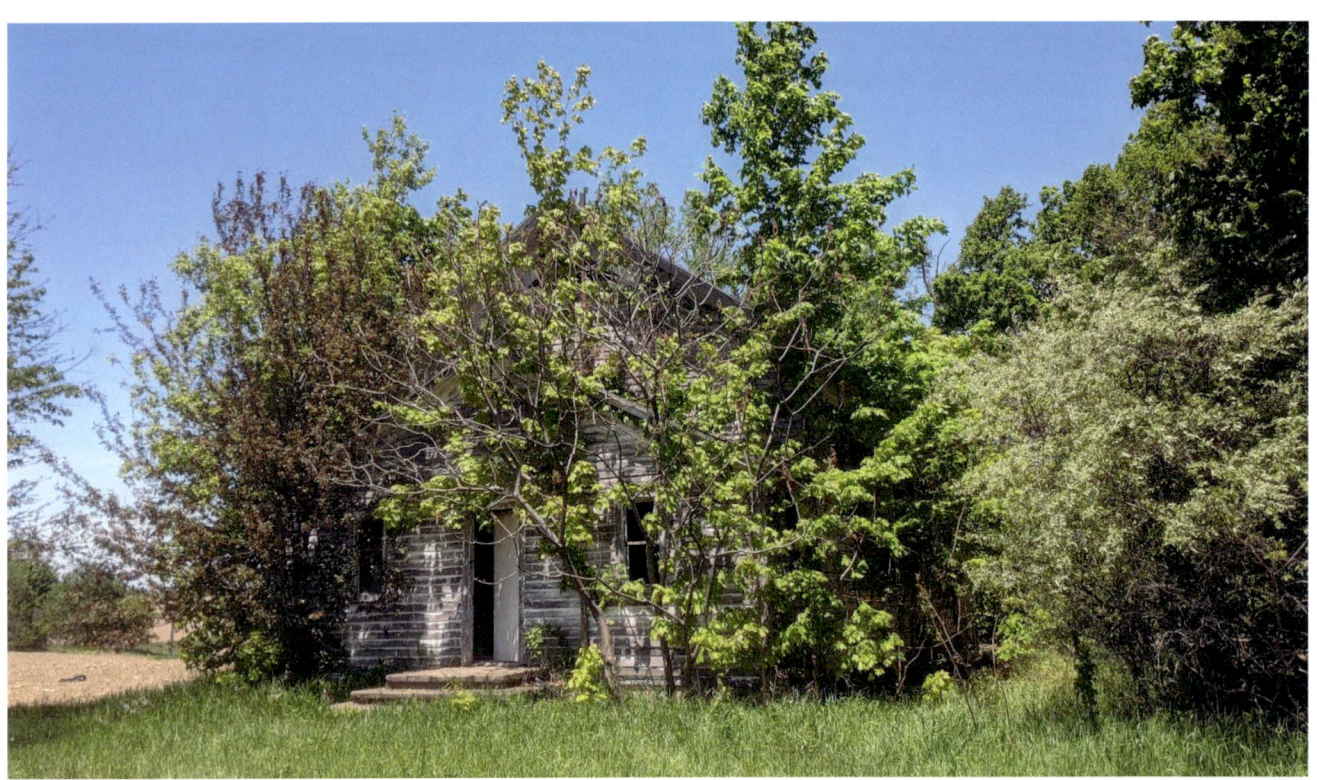

Jamestown High School, Jamestown Township District #2, Section 15, SE corner Riley & 24th
Under construction, 1919

Forest Grove School, Jamestown Township, Section 20, NW corner Perry & 32nd, circa 1900

Forest Grove Elementary School, Jamestown Township , Section 20, NW corner Perry & 32nd, May 2020

Mitchell School, Jamestown Township, Section 24, SE corner Adams & 8th, 2020

Hilzey School, Jamestown Township, Section 25, NE corner Perry & 8th

(Unidentified School), Jamestown Township, Section 30, E side 48th S of Perry, May 2020

Gitchel School, Jamestown Township District #6, Section 33, SW corner Adams & 24th, May 2020

Olive (and future Port Sheldon) Township, 1912

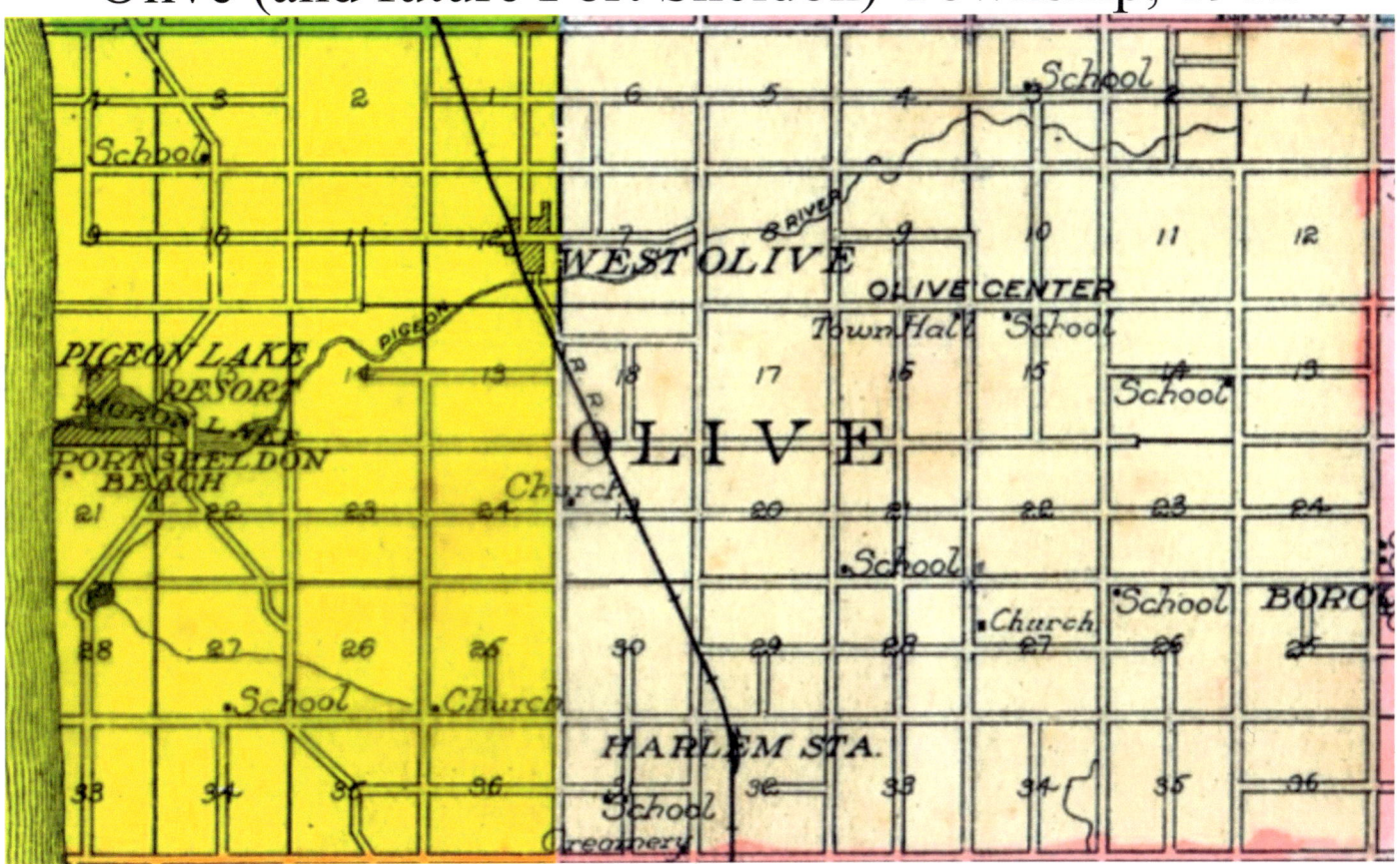

Port Sheldon Township (highlighted in yellow) was officially organized April 7, 1924, breaking away from Olive Township. The majority of residents felt they were not being properly represented, since Township officials were from the more heavily populated eastern farm area.
Source: https://www.portsheldontwp.org/history

Olive Township Schools

School Name	District	Section	Location	Notes
Blendon Station?		21	NE cor Port Sheldon & 128th (1912 map)	Presumed school name based on proximity to extinct village of Blendon Station; No longer standing
Connell		11 (Now in Port Sheldon Twp)	NE cor Croswell & 160th (1876 map)	Built in 1874, this one-room schoolhouse was named for John Connell [O'Connell] family. School records go back to 1865. The first teacher was Anna Gibbs of Crockery Township. She later married Samuel Dell; Schoolhouse status unknown
Groenewault?		26	SE cor Port Sheldon & 112th (1912 map)	Presumed school name based on surrounding Groenewault property on 1876 map; No longer standing
North Holland Station?		31	S side Barry W of 140th (1912 map)	Presumed school name based on proximity to extinct village of North Holland Station on 1876 map; Now Christian Fellowship Center
Ottawa Station	1	3	N side Stanton Rd @ 116th	Built in 1867, moved in 1876, closed in 1958; Now a museum
Olive Center		15	SW cor Polk & 116th (1912 map)	No longer standing

Oven		14	SW cor Baldwin & 104th (1912 map)	Previously presumed to be Webster School based on surrounding Webster property on 1876 map; Converted to residence
West Olive		12 (Now in Port Sheldon Twp)	West Olive village	Built in 1863; Destroyed by fire Jan 16, 1953; New school dedicated Mar 1954

Ottawa Station School, Olive Township District #1, Section 3, N side Stanton Rd @ 116th

Oven School, Olive Township, Section 14, SW corner Baldwin & 104th

North Holland Station School? Olive Township, Section 31, S side Barry W of 140th

Holland (and future Park) Township, 1912

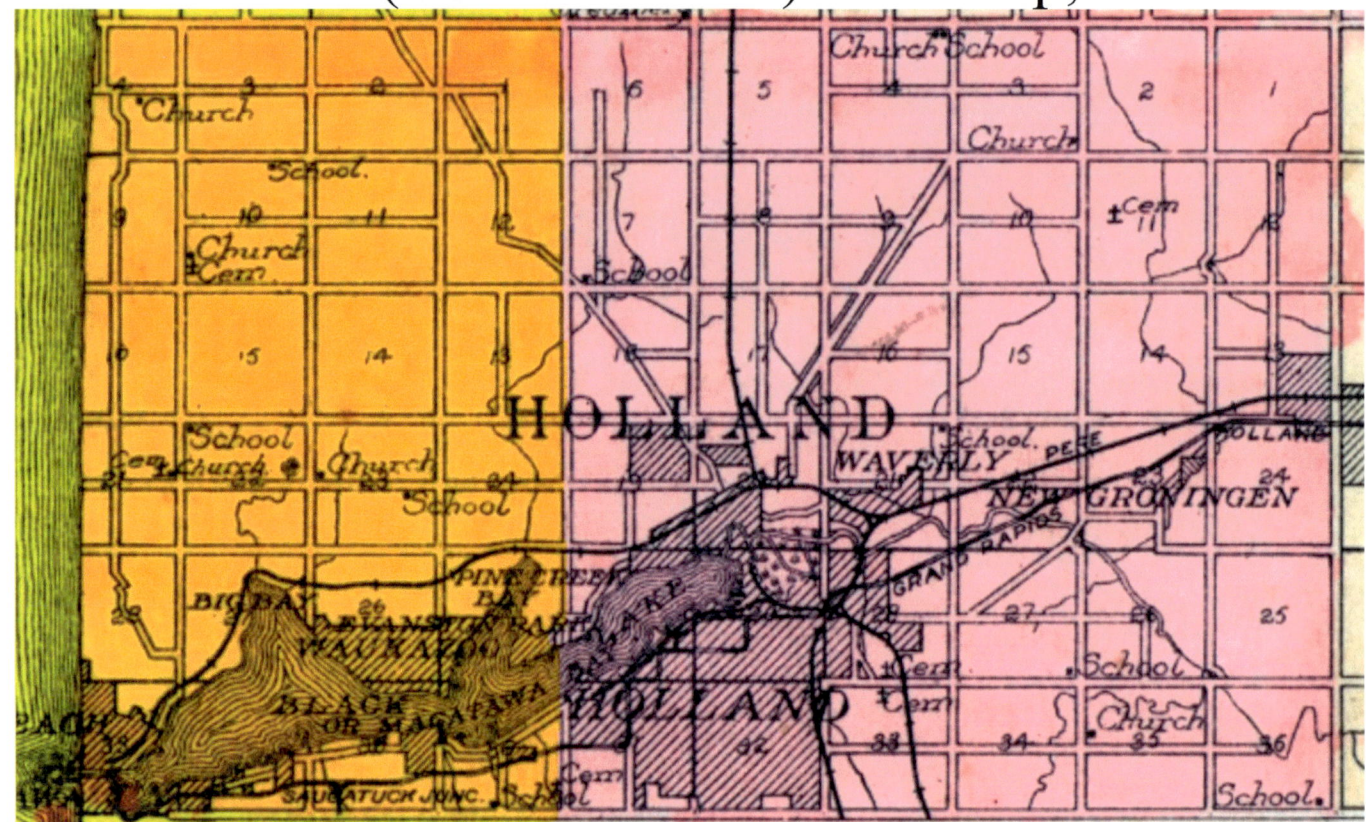

Park Township (highlighted in yellow) was officially organized in 1915, breaking away from Holland Township.

Park Township Schools

School Name	District	Section	Location	Notes
		3	N side Quincy ¼ mi E of 168th	No longer standing
		4	SW cor Ransom & 168th (1876 map)	No longer standing
Lakeshore Elementary		9	168th Av S of Quincy	West Ottawa School District
		10	S side Quincy ½ mi E of 168th (1912 map)	No longer standing
Lakewood Elementary		21	SW cor Lakewood & 168th	West Ottawa School District
		22	SE cor James & 168th (1912 map)	No longer standing
Waukazoo Elementary		23	S side Lakewood ¼ mi W of 152nd, Holland	West Ottawa School District
		36	NW cor 32nd & Lugers/Luggers (1912 map)	No longer standing

Lakeshore Elementary School, Park Township, Section 9, 168ᵗʰ Av S of Quincy

Waukazoo Elementary School, West Ottawa Schools, Park Twp, Sec 23, S side Lakewood ¼ mi W of 152nd

Polkton Township, 1912

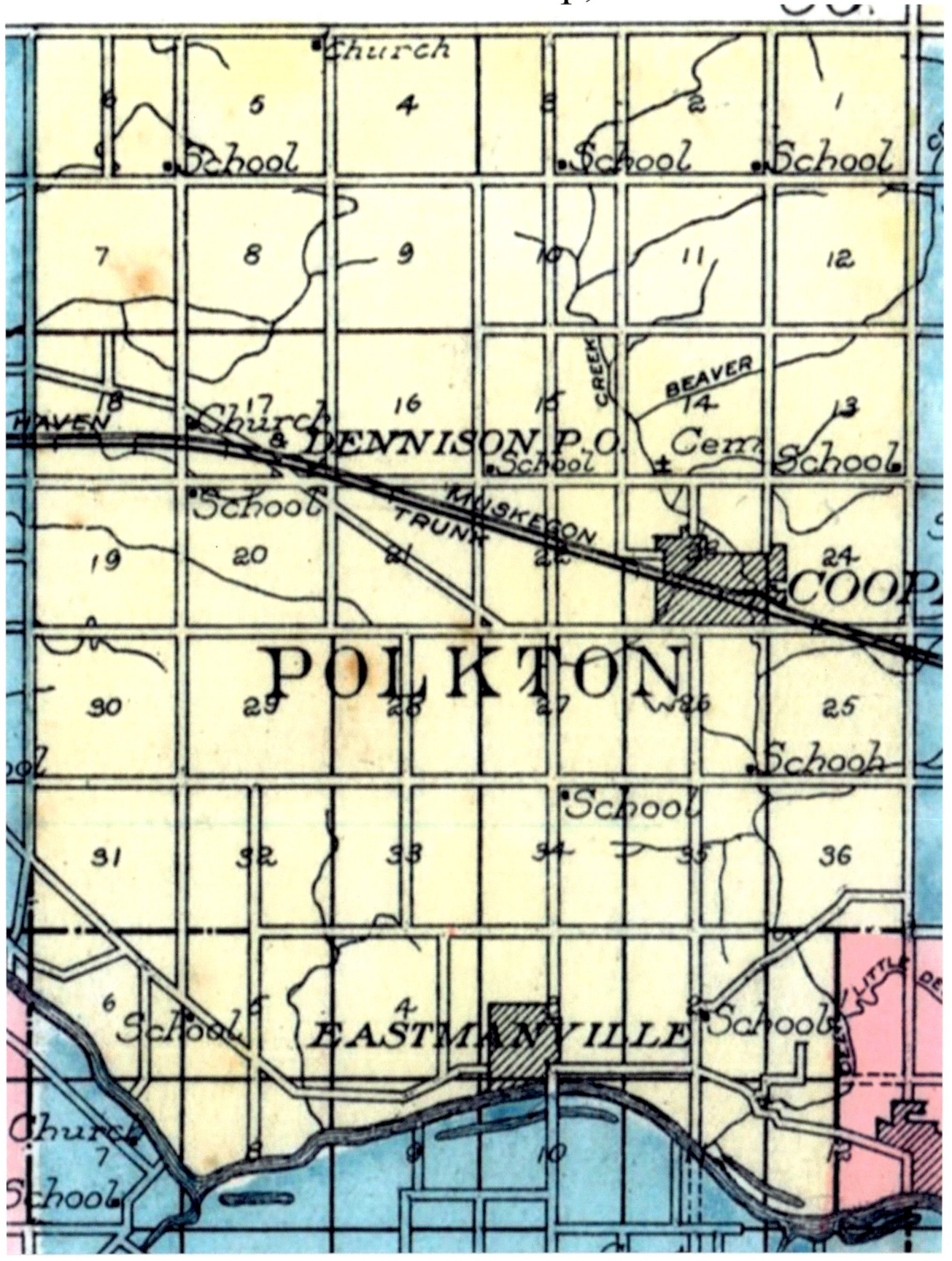

Polkton Township Schools

School Name	District	Section	Location	Notes
Cooper		1(N)	NW cor Taft & 56th	In June 1885, Cooper School District was formed north of Coopersville; 1st classes were in a log building; A new schoolhouse was built in 1886, with a basement & annex added later; Converted to residence
North Evergreen		3(N)	SE cor Taft & 72nd (1912 map)	Nellie Mulder, teacher, Aug 28, 1936; Converted to residence
Jericho	5	6(N)	NW cor Taft & 88th (1912 map)	Built in 1854; A new building was constructed in 1926 for $4,000; Closed in 1960, students sent to the Coopersville Schools. Helen Shaw, teacher, Aug 28, 1936; Renovation in progress
Red / "The Little Red Schoolhouse"		2(S)	SE cor Mill Rd & 60th Av (1912 map)	Fenno Densmore, teacher, Aug 28, 1936; Converted to residence
South Evergreen	7	5(S)	SW side Leonard E of 88th (1912 map)	Marjorie Piper, teacher, Aug 28, 1936; Still standing
Centennial	8	2	NW cor Taft & 56th (1912 map)	1907-1958; On December 5, 1845, the State of Michigan conveyed a parcel of land to George S. Lovett who kept the ground in 1865 when the land was sold to Tolford Durham with the understanding that the land be used for school purposes only. The Charles Durham family transferred the ½ acre to the school board of School District #8 on August 14, 1907, and the school remained in session until 1958 when the district was joined with the Coopersville Public Schools. The white building at the NW corner of 56th Avenue and Taft stood as a landmark until 1994 when the building was burned; Asa Kelly, teacher, Aug 28, 1936
Eastmanville / Polkton	1	3	NE cor Leonard & 68th; Eastmanville	In 1842, Eastmanville, Polkton School Dist #1 organized as Tallmadge Township, originally encompassing Allendale and Polkton Townships; 1st log school was built in 1842; 2nd school was completed January 1, 1849; Rebuilt in 1926 with addition dedicated December 14, 1928; June Witcop, teacher, Aug 28, 1936
The Little School		23	333 Ottawa St, Coopersville	Used mainly for kindergarten, 1st & 2nd grades in early 1900s; Once served as American Legion post; Now site of Coopersville Area District Library
Coopersville East Elementary		24	198 East St (Campus Dr), Coopersville	
Coopersville High		24	198 East St (Campus Dr), Coopersville	Charles D. Veldhuis, superintendent, Aug 28, 1936
Coopersville Middle		24	198 East St (Campus Dr), Coopersville	
Jackson	1F	24	785 Cleveland Rd; NW cor Cleveland & 48th	Mrs. Matilda Dyke, teacher, Aug 28, 1936; Torn down and replaced by house
Coopersville South Elementary		24	198 East St (Campus Dr), Coopersville	
Rankin	2	26	N side Garfield E of 60th	1st school built in 1841; Current structure built in 1890; William Stiles as the first teacher; Mrs. Dorothy Vandermate, teacher, Aug 28, 1936; Converted to residence
Hanchett				

| Marshall | 5 | | Near Cleveland & 52nd | In 1851, classes were held in a lean-to building off the F. A. Marshall home. A wood frame building was erected in 1855 near Cleveland and 72nd Avenue at a cost of $440. In 1906 a cement block building was constructed to replace the frame one. This burned, and a second cement block building was erected which was much like the first one and still stands today; The first teacher, Mary Ann Murphy, earned $2.00 per week, and out of that salary she paid $1.00 a week for room and board to the family where she stayed. Many of the teachers lived with a family in the area due to poor transportation. Marshall School joined the Coopersville Public Schools in 1960; Mrs. Hester Ruster, teacher, Aug 28, 1936; No longer standing |
| Toothacre | | | | Mrs. C. Sikkema, teacher, Aug 28, 1936 |

The Little School (as the American Legion post), Polkton Township, 333 Ottawa, Cooperstown

Centennial School, 1909, Polkton Towship, District #8, Section 2, NW corner Taft & 56th

Jackson School, Polkton Township, Fractional District 1F, 785 Cleveland Rd; NW cor Cleveland & 48th

"The Little Red Schoolhouse", Polkton Township, Section 2(S), SE cor 60th & Mill

North Evergreen School, Polkton Township, Section 3, NE corner Taft & 68th

South Evergreen School, Polkton Township, District 7, Section 5(S), SW side Leonard E of 88th

Jericho School, circa 1900, Polkton Township, Section 9, NW corner Taft & 88th

Jericho School, May 2020, Polkton Township, Section 9, NW cornerTaft & 88th, 1900

Jericho School, May 2020, Polkton Township, Section 9, NW cornerTaft & 88th, 2020

Rankin School, date unknown, Polkton Township, District #2, Section 26, N side Garfield E of 60th

Rankin School, May 2020, Polkton Township, District #2, Section 26, N side Garfield E of 60th

Port Sheldon Township, 1912
(then part of Olive Township)

Port Sheldon Township was officially organized April 7, 1924, breaking away from Olive Township. The majority of residents felt they were not being properly represented, since Township officials were from the more heavily populated eastern farm area.

Source: https://www.portsheldontwp.org/history

School Name	District	Section	Location	Notes
		3	NW cor Croswell & 164th/Hiawatha (1912 map)	No longer standing
Connell		11	NE cor Croswell & 160th (1876 map, Olive Twp)	Built in 1874, this one-room schoolhouse was named for John Connell [O'Connell] family. School records go back to 1865. The first teacher was Anna Gibbs of Crockery Township. She later married Samuel Dell; Schoolhouse status unknown; Irish name likely changed due to prejudice against Irish.
West Olive		12	Village of West Olive	Built in 1863; Destroyed by fire Jan 16, 1953; New school dedicated Mar 1954
Sheldon Woods Elementary		24	15050 Blair St, West Olive; S side Blair St E of 152nd Av	Opened in 1965; Dedicated Apr 12, 1966
		24	E side 152nd betw Blair & West Olive	Now Iglesia de Dios Septima Dia (House of God Seventh Day Church)
Smith		27	NE cor Van Buren & Butternut	Built in 1870; Named for Richard Smith family; New building erected in 1885-86 with older structure used to store firewood; No longer standing
Robar		22	N side Port Sheldon St W of 160th, 16200 Port Sheldon St, West Olive	Considered 1st school in Port Sheldon Twp (originally part of Olive Twp), named after John C. Robar family; Converted to church in early 1900s, and township hall in 1924; Replaced by modern township hall
Pigeon Creek	3	34	SE cor Pierce St & 168th Av	1st school, School District No. 3, was a log building built in 1869 in an Indian settlement north of Pigeon Creek; 2nd school, Pigeon Creek School, was built in 1878 and is still standing after being moved, then returned to its original site in 2007 by the Pigeon Creek Schoolhouse Preservation Society

Site of Robar School, Port Sheldon Township, Section 22, N side Port Sheldon St W of 160th, now Port Sheldon Township Hall, 16200 Port Sheldon St, West Olive

(Unidentified School), Port Sheldon Township, Section 24, E side 152nd N of Blair,
Iglesia de Dios Septima Dia (House of God of Seventh Day)

Sheldon Woods Elementary School, West Ottawa Public Schools, Port Sheldon Township, Section 24, S side
Blair E of 152nd

Robinson Township, 1912

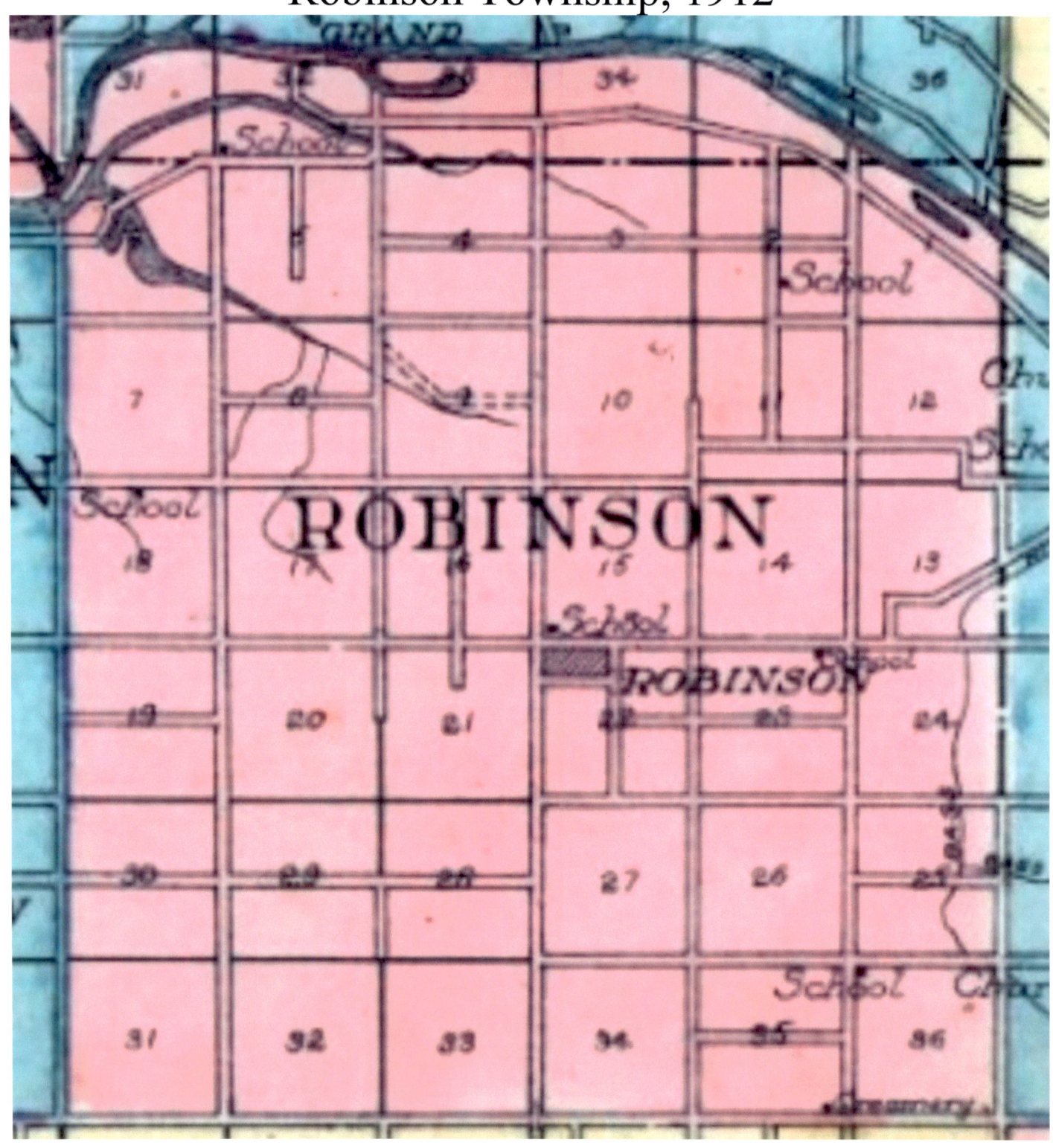

Robinson Township Schools

School Name	District	Section	Location	Notes
North Robinson	1		108th Av betw Sleeper & Johnson, Grand Haven	Joan Parker, teacher, Aug 28, 1936
Maplewood	2	31(S)	SW cor 120th Av & Buchanan St	Still standing as of 1996, now gone; Evelyn Antes, teacher, Aug 28, 1936
Clark (1st schoolhouse)	3	7	E side 144th Av, approx. 1 mi S of Green St	Log structure built in 1864 was converted into Clark School; New frame structure built in 1869, moved to Green Street near Stearn's Bayou.
Clark (2nd schoolhouse)	3	32(N)	N side Hayes & 136th near Stearns Bayou	Moved from 144th in 1875; Operated until 1914 when part was moved to Felix's Marina and converted to residence; Remaining structure continued operation as school until 1958 when it was also converted to residence; Helen Clark, teacher, Aug 28, 1936
Robinson Center	4		Buchanan E of 120th, Grand Haven	Theressa Shaarda, teacher, Aug 28, 1936
Knight	5	18	S side Lincoln E of 144th	Named for landowner James W. Knight who owned 92 acres in Section 18; operated from 1886 until 1913 when West Robinson opened on 136th S of Lincoln; No longer standing
Robinson	5	15	11801 120th Av, Grand Haven; NE cor 120th Av & Buchanan St (1912 map)	Replaced by modern facility, now an elementary school
West Robinson	5	18	W side 136th S of Lincoln	Built in 1913 to replace Knight School; Ceased operation in 1958; No longer standing
New Era	6		104th Av S of Pierce, Zeeland	Converted to storage barn
Worley	7	28	E side 128th ¼ mi S of Winans	1915-1958; Helen L. Price, teacher, Aug 28, 1936; Torn down
		2	E side 108th ¼ mi N of Johnson (1912 map)	No longer standing
		17	SW cor Lincoln & 144th (1912 map)	
		23	SW cor Buchanan & 104th (1912 map)	No longer standing
		32(S)	SW cor Lincoln & 128th	Unconfirmed; Converted to residence
		36(S)	SE cor Pierce & 104th (1912 map)	No longer standing

The original North Robinson School was built in 1851 at 104th Avenue between North Cedar Drive and 10rth Avenue, then later to the 108th Avenue site, which is where this photo was taken. I am unsure whehter the building was moved or if new structures were built. Like six of the seven Robinson Township schoolhouses, use was discontinued in 1958 when the district consolidated. It became a private residence for a a decade or so before being demolished and a geodesic dome house was constructed on the site. - Betsy Cech

Maplewood School, Robinson Township District 2

The original District 2 school was built in 1857 and was called Barnard School as it was located at Barnard Corners. It burned in 1920, was rebuilt at the same location, and was then called Maplewood School. During its construction, the students attended school in the nearby Grange Hall. Use was discontinued with consolidation in 1958 - Betty Cech

Clark School, Robinson Township, Section 32(N), N side Hayes & 136th near Stearns Bayou

Clark School started life in 1864 as a log buildin on 144th Avenue between Johnson Street and Lincoln Street. In 1875, it was moved across the old Rogers Bridge at the back of Stearn's Bayou to its present location. Clark School has had numerous additions over the years, with the largest one added in 1949. When the Robinson Districts consolidated, Clark School continued to be used for a few year for Special Education classes. - Betsy Cech

Robinson Center School, Robinson Township District 3

This 1874 school was built on land said to have been donated by Mrs. Fisher of Robinson village. As with most Robinson Township schools, it closed in 1958 when Robinson Consolidated School opened. - Betty Cech

Knight School, Robinson Township District 5

The original 1884 District 5 schoolhouse was called Knight School because it was located on the J. W. Knight property, closer to the corner of 144th and Lincoln. In 1914, a new district 5 school was constructed on 136th, and the name was changed to West Robinson School. It was used until district consolidation in 1858. When the former Knight School was razed or moved is unknown - Betty Cech

West Robinson School, Robinson Township District 5

The original 1884 District 5 schoolhouse was called Knight School because of its location on J. W. Knight's property. In 1914, a new district 5 schoolhouse was constructed on 138th, and the name was changed to West Robinson School. - Betty Cech

Robinson Elementary School, Robinson Township, Section 21, W side 120th @ Pingree

New Era School, in southern Robinson Township was built in 1889 and discontinue in 1958 with the consolidation of Robinson Schools. In 1960, former student James VanderKooi purchased the schoolhouse and moved in a half mile to his blueberry farm on Pierce Street between 112th and 104th Avenues. It was set on a basement in which blueberry sorting, cleaning and packaging occurred. In 1967, James' son John purchased the farm. He and his wife lived on the main floor of the old schoolhouse during the growing season. From 1974 to the present, the building has been used for storage. - Betty Cech

Worley School, Robinson Township District 7

Worley School was opened in 1915 on land donated by R. F. Worley. It had only four students the first year and continued to have so few students that it closed for a few years in the 1940s. It has since been demolished. - Betty Cech

Unidentified School? Robinson Township, Section 32(S), SW corner Lincoln & 128th

Spring Lake Township, 1912

Spring Lake Township Schools

		4	NW cor Taft & 168th (1912 map)	No longer standing
DeWitt	6	8	17716 W Taft Rd; S side Taft ¼ mi E of 180th	1891 – 1957; Designated a National Historic Site
Jeffers		24	14429 Leonard; NW cor Leonard & 144th	Built in 1868; Original building converted to residence before being replaced by the current Jeffers Elementary School
Barber Street / Barber			102 W. Exchange St; SW cor Park St & Mason St, Spring Lake (Mill Point)	Built prior to 1844, rebuilt, renovated, and twice relocated; Now stands (as Barber School) on SW cor Buchanan & Exchange as Community Building
St. Mary's Catholic			200 Prospect St, Spring Lake; NE cor Exchange & Prospect	Still in operation
Union			Exchange St, Spring Lake (exact location not specified)	Built in 1869; North wing added in 1880; Destroyed by fire May 11, 1893; Replaced in 1894 by a brick building; Replaced by Holmes School in 1951
Central			NE cor Exchange & Buchanan	2-Story brick building built in 1893-94 to replace Union School that burned down May 11, 1893; Site is now a parking lot
Ferrysburg	1		Elm St, Ferrysburg	District #1 organized in 1857; 1st school was wooden structure painted white, enlarged as attendance grew; Two-story structure replaced it in 1927 just north of old school; Extensively damaged by fire Feb 10, 1953; Replaced by one-story brick building in September 1954; Still stands as a business
Holmes Elementary			426 River St, Spring Lake	Replaced Central School on corner of Buchanan & Exchange Streets; still in operation
Park Street			400 Liberty St, Spring Lake; SE cor Liberty & Park	Property for school purchased November 3, 1854; Now occupied by red brick house
Spring Lake Jr/Sr High			345 Hammond St, Spring Lake; SE cor South St & Hammond St	Opened in 1959; New high school built at 16140 148th Av in Fall 2000; Still in operation as Spring Lake Middle School

Ferrysburg School, Spring Lake Township, Elm St, Ferrysburg

Holmes Elementary School, Spring Lake Township, 426 River St, Spring Lake

Barber Street School, Spring Lake Township; 102 W Exchange St; SW corner Park St & Mason St
Spring Lake (previously known as Mill Point)

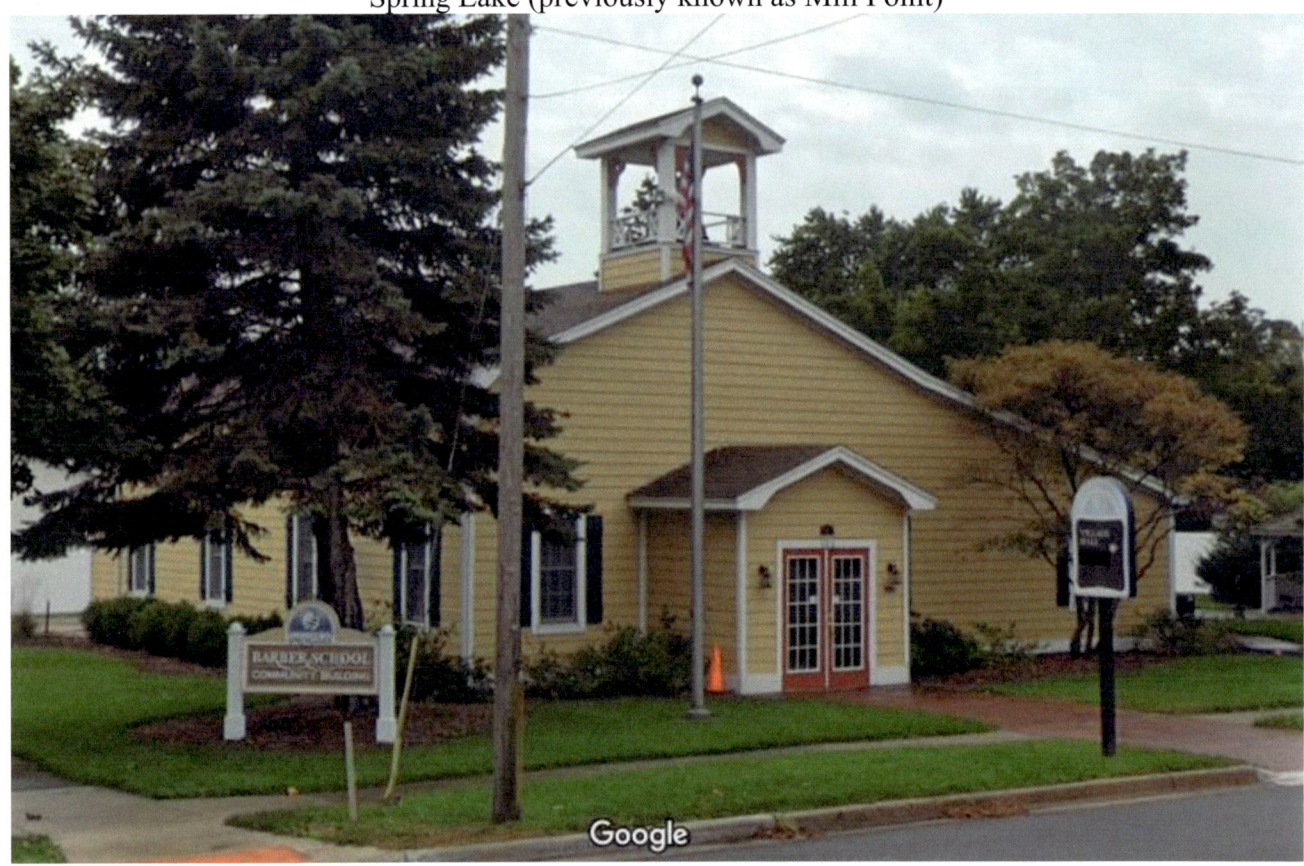

DeWitt School, Spring Lake Township, District #6, Section 8, S side Taft Rd; 17716 Taft Rd, Spring Lake

DEWITT SCHOOL

Built in 1891, DeWitt School typifies the one-room schools of the turn of the century. It stands on an acre of land that was donated by the DeWitt and Bosch families. Classes for grades one through eight were held in it until 1957. At one time, a single teacher taught from twenty-five to forty students by holding one ten-minute session per subject for each of the eight grades. The original school district covered approximately four square miles, and many children walked more than two miles to and from school daily. Nearly two decades after the school closed, planning began for restoring it as a living museum for area school children. By 1979 the classroom resembled its 1891 appearance, featuring gas lights, a wood stove, an octagonal clock, a hanging globe, lunch pails and desks.

MICHIGAN HISTORY DIVISION, DEPARTMENT OF STATE
REGISTERED LOCAL SITE NO. 640
PROPERTY OF THE STATE OF MICHIGAN, 1982

Jeffers Elementary School, Spring Lake Township, Section 24, NW corner Leonard & 144th

Spring Lake School, Spring Lake Township, circa 1950

Spring Lake School Complex, including Holmes Elementary School, Spring Lake Intermediate School, Spring Lake Middle School, and Spring Lake High School football field

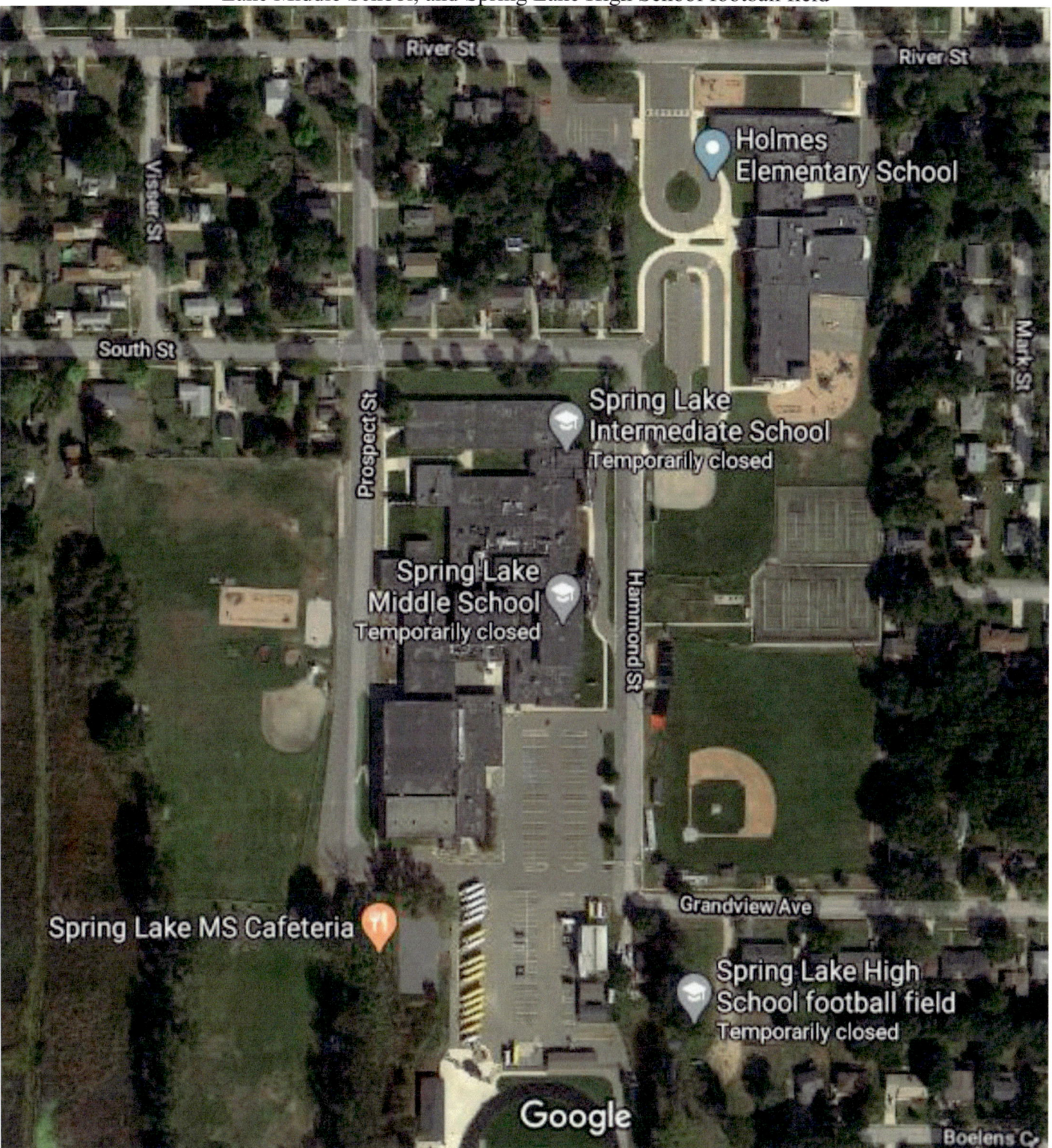

Site of Park Street School, Spring Lake Twp, SE corner Liberty & Park, Spring Lake

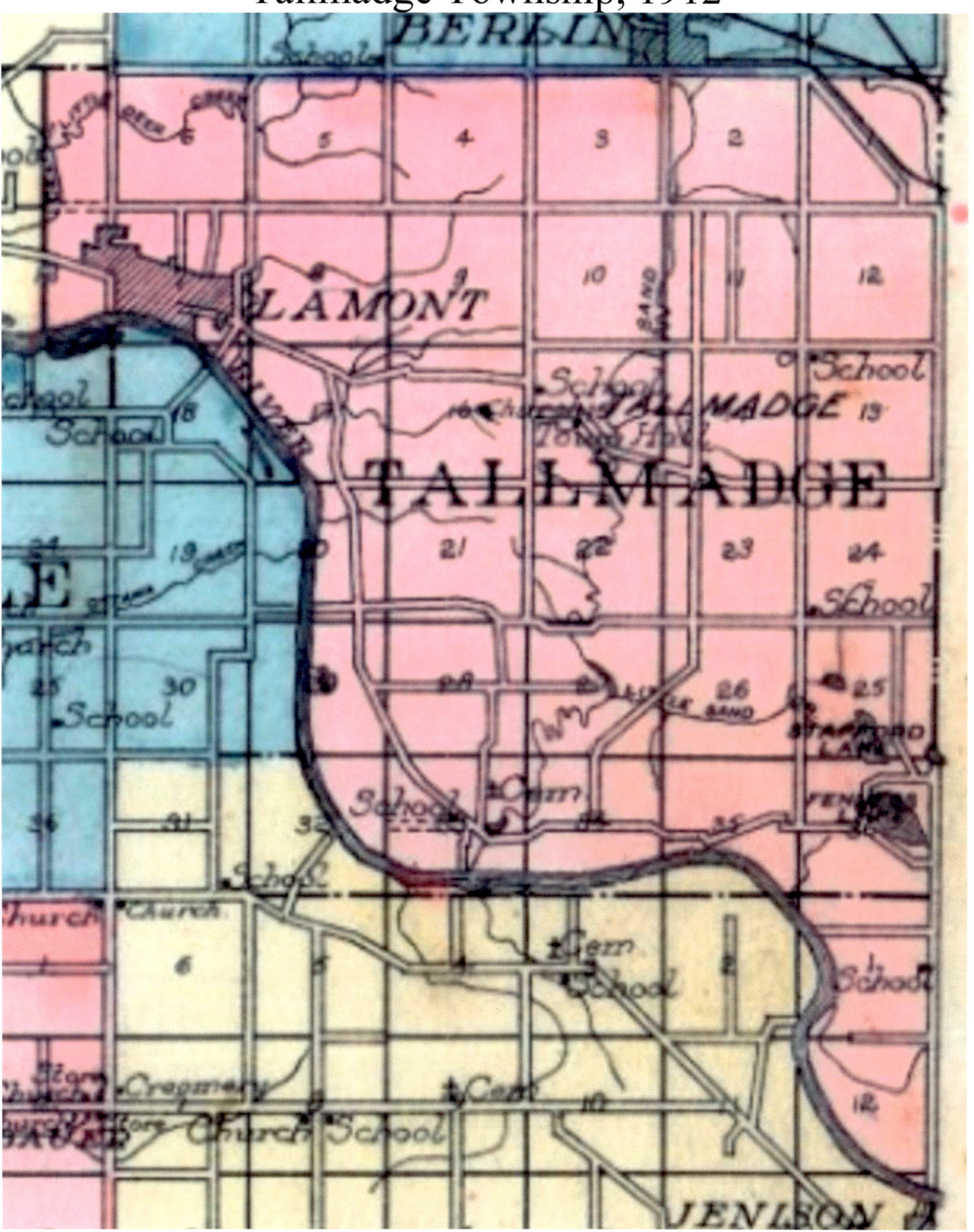

Tallmadge Township Schools

School Name	District	Section	Location	Notes
Lamont Christian		12	5260 Leonard, Marne	Currently operating
Star	5	13	SE cor Lincoln & 8th	1853 - Built on corner of 8th Avenue and Johnson Street 1869 - Moved to corner of 8th Avenue and Lincoln Street 1972 - Moved to Blandford Nature Center, Grand Rapids
Red		15	NE cor Leonard & 24th	Burned down circa 1912
Cross	3	15	NE cor Leonard & 24th	Built in 1913 after previous Red School burned down; Torn down in 1960; Morris E. Kronemeyer, teacher, Aug 28, 1936
Tallmadge		15	E side 24th @ Leonard (1912 map)	No longer standing
		24	NE cor Lake Michigan Dr & 8th (1912 map)	Now Future Steps Pre-School
River Bend	10F	1(S)	W side Kenowa Av @ Riverbend Dr (1912 map)	Yellow brick Schoolhouse built in 1878; Replaced in 1952 by present building; Students now attend Grandville Schools; Frank Clark, teacher, Aug 28, 1936
Delaney	4			Jessie Doane, teacher, Aug 28, 1936
Lamont High	1		Lamont	Martin Bouwma, principal; Mrs. Alice Smith, teacher, Aug 28, 1936
Lamont – Steele's Landing	1			Location and status unknown
Baxter	2			Location and status unknown
Luther	3F			Location and status unknown
Harris	6			Location and status unknown
Coombs – Blakeney	7			Location and status unknown
Sand Creek	8			Location and status unknown

Lamont Christian School, 5275 Leonard St, Marne, Tallmadge Twp, Section 12

Riverbend Elementary School, Tallmadge Township, Section 1(South), W side Kenowa @ Riverbend

Star School, Tallmadge Township, Section 13, SE corner Lincoln & 8th, (now @ Blandford Nature Center)

Cross School, 1913, Tallmadge Township, Section 15, NE corner Leonard & 24th

Wright Township, 1912

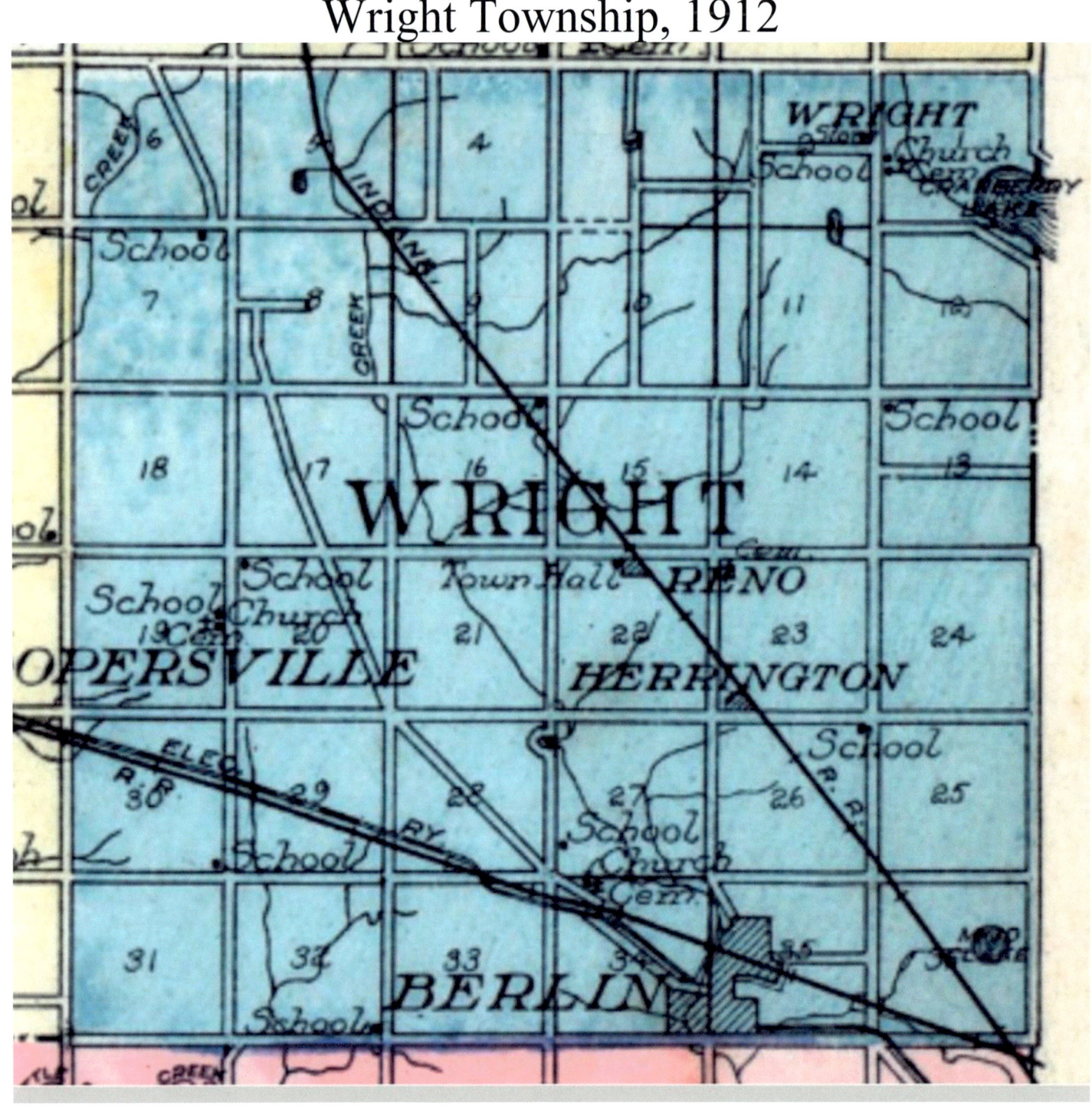

Wright Township Schools

School Name	District	Section	Location	Notes
Boody	?	7	S side Taft @ Elder Dr (1912 map)	On Geo. Boody's 75 acres; Mrs. Agnes VanWiltenberg, teacher, Aug 28, 1936; No longer standing
Brown?	?	13	SE cor Roosevelt & 8th (1912 map)	on Peter Brown's 219 acres; No longer standing
Wolverton?	?	16	SW cor Roosevelt & 24th (1912 map)	on Chas. Wolverton's 116 acres; No longer standing
Wright	?	19	W side 40th betw Cleveland & Arthur (1912 map)	On J. E. Root's 27 acres; Now part of Wright Seventh Day Adventist Church
Palmatier?	?	20	SE cor Cleveland & 40th (1912 map)	On Jesse Palmatier's 39 acres; Converted to residence
Gillett?	?	26	SW cor Arthur & 8th (1912 map)	On Alva Gillett's 80-acre Maple Row Farm; Converted to residence
Farrel?	?	27	E side 24th ½ mi N of Juniper (1912 map)	On Jos. Farrel's 120 acres; No longer standing
Mohn?	?	30	NW cor Garfield & 40th (1912 map)	On F.J. Mohn's 40 acres; Possibly still standing
Lillie	?	32	NW cor Hayes & 32nd (1912 map)	On C.C. Lillie's 40 acres; Mrs. Vera E. Bliss, teacher, Aug 28, 1936; No longer standing
Clayton	?	?	?	Mrs. Louise Gahan, teacher, Aug 28, 1936
McDearmen	?	?	?	Frank Clark, teacher, Aug 28, 1936

Wright School and Church, Wright Township, Section 19, W side 40th between Cleveland & Arthur (via Google 3D)

Wright School, Wright Township, Section 19, W side 40th between Cleveland & Arthur, May 2020

Gillett School? Wright Township, Section 26, SW corner Arthur & 8th, May 2020

Zeeland Township, 1912

Zeeland Township Schools

School Name	District	Section	Location	Notes
		5	NW cor Quincy & 80th (1912 map)	Converted to residence
Indian Creek		11	3585 56th Street, Hudsonville; W side 56th Av betw Riley & Quincy	Contact: Mitch Berkenpas (mitch@accn.org); Converted to residence
Vriesland		22	SW cor Byron & 64th, Vriesland (1912 map)	No longer standing
West Drenthe		28	NW cor Adams & 78th	Moved to 428 W Fennville Rd, Fennville, Allegan County
		35	SE cor Adams & 64th (1912 map)	No longer standing

Zeeland's first Grade School, 1879

Zeeland High School graduates, 1898

Standing: James C. DePree, Susan Noordhof, Sadie Cass, Kate Everhard (one name missing)
Seated: Gertrude VanLoo, Jacob Elenbaas, George Rookus, Principal Charles Cogshall, and Bertha Veneklasen

Zeeland High School 8th Grade graduates, 1917

Seated: Josie Zuverink, Tessie Luidens Bouma, Henry Arends, Antoinette Northuis, Anna Terpstra
Standing: Theodore VanDyke, Winnie Jeigersma, Marguerite Wiersma, Marian VandenBosch, Sena Telgenhof, Anna Telgenhof, Ella VanOmmen, William Staal

For further study and research:

Tri-Cities Historical Society
1 North Harbor Drive
Grand Haven, MI 49417
616-842-0700

Holland Area Historical Society @ Hope College
9 East Tenth Street
Holland, MI 49423
616-395-7798

Coopersville Area Historical Society
363 Main Street
Coopersville, MI 49404
616-997-7240

Made in United States
Cleveland, OH
11 July 2025

18448124R00067